K. A. BUSIA ON AFRICA

Volume 3

AFRICA IN SEARCH OF DEMOCRACY

AFRICA IN SEARCH
OF DEMOCRACY

K. A. BUSIA

Published in cooperation with
BFI in celebration of its silver anniversary

First published in 1967 by Routledge & Kegan Paul Ltd

This edition first published in 2023
by Routledge
4 Park Square, Milton Park, Abingdon, Oxon OX14 4RN

and by Routledge
605 Third Avenue, New York, NY 10158

Routledge is an imprint of the Taylor & Francis Group, an informa business

British Library Cataloguing in Publication Data
A catalogue record for this book is available from the British Library

ISBN: 978-1-032-32672-6 (Set)
ISBN: 978-1-032-19670-1 (Volume 3) (hbk)
ISBN: 978-1-032-19678-7 (Volume 3) (pbk)
ISBN: 978-1-003-26029-5 (Volume 3) (ebk)

DOI: 10.4324/9781003260295

Publisher's Note
The publisher has gone to great lengths to ensure the quality of this reprint but points out that some imperfections in the original copies may be apparent.

Disclaimer
The publisher has made every effort to trace copyright holders and would welcome correspondence from those they have been unable to trace.

New Introduction to the Reissue of 2023

Address at Runnymede on 15 June 1965 Commemoration of Magna Carta. Society for Individual Freedom

I deem it a great honour to have been invited to speak here at Runnymede, on this thrilling occasion, commemorating one of the most historic events of British history – the signing of Magna Carta here, 750 years ago.

Even though I am an African, it gives me pleasure to be here to take part in these celebrations, for we commemorate an event which belongs not only to Britain, but also to the Commonwealth, and indeed to all mankind, there are certain ideas and achievements of man which become the heritage not only of the countries where they originate, but of all mankind. Magna Carta is one of them. It not only gave expression to ideas which led to democratic rule in these islands, but it has also become a symbol of human freedom and dignity; and of democratic government under the rule of law; a symbol of that true democracy which recognizes the worth and dignity of every human being as a unique person, whatever his creed or colour or country.

Magna Carta did more than kindle the struggle for basic human rights and the dignity of the individual. In the drama that was enacted here at Runnymede, 750 years ago, was portrayed a persistent and universal problem of man in society: the problem of how those who wield power should be controlled by those over whom they rule. It is a universal human experience that those who rule are prone to act without due consideration of what they are doing to others;

they tend to be corrupted by power. Those who are ruled must have an effective way of checking the excesses of their rulers. For all free men everywhere, power must be subject to law. This is one of the notable lessons of the drama of Runnymede. The barons who gathered here 750 years ago were men who had grievances; have ideas and visions. The barons were men who not only claimed, but also exercised the right of people with grievances to get together at public meetings to discuss and to agitate for what they think is the right course in public affairs. Government by consent means individuals must be able to group together and be able to make their voices heard through their groups. The freedoms of association and of speech are fundamental freedoms for all free men. Would-be authoritarian and despotic rulers have always been tempted to curb them.

More than this, some of the clauses of Magna Carta remind us of the cardinal principle of natural justice; that no one should have a case against him decided without an opportunity of presenting his side of the case at a fair trial. There should always be impartial courts to give protection to personal liberties.

While we meet here at this place, hallowed as the birthplace of high principles of personal liberties, and high ideals of the dignity of the individual, it behaves us to remember that there are many countries in the world today where the foundations of individual freedom are being undermined.

I regret to say my own country of Ghana is among them. There, President Nkrumah's government has become an indefensible tyranny. The President has put himself above the law; checks on the exercise of his powers have been eroded; and the rule of law has been violated. He has reduced elections to a farce, and the people have lost any effective power to elect and remove their legislators and rulers; the courts have been rendered powerless to deny the President the right he has assumed to imprison a citizen arbitrarily, without a fair trial. The argument that seeks to justify all this on the grounds of economic development is vitiated; facts have belied theory; there is increasing economic hardship for the many and luxurious comfort for the few; public funds have been spent on palaces and prestige projects, on spies, and police and bodyguards; and on intrigues against neighbouring countries. There is no freedom of speech or association. All who attempt to voice grievances, as the barons did here 750 years ago, are in danger of arbitrary arrest and imprisonment; the jails have filled up; and refugees have fled abroad. The danger of arrest and imprisonment and even torture that faces anyone who does or says anything that the government does not like, has threatened all other freedoms. This pattern of development down the path of tyranny is a familiar one.

Many countries have been known to travel along it. Because of this, there are some who have sought persuasively to condone injustice and tyranny; but the arguments they have advanced seem to set up one standard of values for whites and another for dark skinned peoples.

All human beings love freedom and justice and abhor tyranny. The history of every country has a record of men who in their day withstood tyrannical acts, just as the barons did here at Runnymede. In towns and villages in Africa, as elsewhere, can be found, in the immortal words of Thomas Gray, many a grave of

'Some village - Hampden that with dauntless breast,
The little tyrant of his fields withstood.'

As in the past, there are men and women who are standing against tyranny, risking imprisonment, persecution, even death. In Africa, the battle for national independence has already many victories to its credit; many new independent states have been born; but the long battle to establish basic human rights and personal liberties within each State has only just begun. It has its fighters; the men and women who share the hopes and visions for the achievement of democratic regimes where there will be constitutional checks on those who rule; where people will have the right to choose their rulers; and where the civil liberties and basic human rights for all will be protected under the rule of law by impartial courts. The institutions in which the different peoples will safeguard these basic liberties and give their expression will indeed vary, according to their historical and social circumstances; but wherever the basic rights themselves are denied, there is always the danger of political instability, and a threat to peace. This is why the denial of basic human rights and civil liberties anywhere must always be the concern of freedom and peace-loving peoples everywhere. Condoning injustice and oppression is a disservice to mankind.

In the memory and in the spirit of Runnymede, may we all derive fresh inspiration and go forward, united by hopes and visions for the freedom of man, and the continuing extension and enlargement of human rights and civil liberties for all peoples everywhere. The future does not lie with the forces of cruel tyranny which some are assiduous to placate, but with the irresistible forces of the spirit struggling for freedom and emancipation. The future lies with the spirit of Runnymede and the principles of Magna Carta which will continue to inspire and strengthen many men and women all over the world, through future years, as they fight against tyranny, and serve the noble cause of personal liberties and the dignity of man.

May I again thank you, the officers and members of the Society for Individual Freedom for inviting me here today to be one of the speakers on this memorable occasion.

Dr K. A. Busia
Leader of the United Party of Ghana in Exile.

A Note on *K.A. Busia on Africa*: An Anniversary Set

The idea for the establishment of the Busia Foundation was conceived of by Mrs. Naa Morkor Abrefa Busia (1924–2010) to honour and perpetuate the memory of her late husband Professor Kofi Abrefa Busia (1913–1978) and remind his communities of his ideas and ideals. Busia had an enthusiastic commitment to democracy as the "moral language" of all humanity and to equality of all persons. It has been observed that Busia's ideas have survived the radical populism of the 1960s, the militarism of the 1970s and the 1980s and emerged vindicated in the 1990s. It was to honour these ideas and ideals, and the way he tried to put them into practice over his short term of office as Prime Minister of the Second Republic that the Busia Foundation was established. The Busia Foundation was formally launched in July 1998 in commemoration of Busia's 85th birthday, with Busia Foundation International established three years later. Among the aims and objectives of the Foundations are to preserve and disseminate Busia's ideas and ideals widely by promoting and fostering his concerns for human rights, and the basic needs of people and civic education through a celebration of their vibrant culture. An anchoring task of this aspiration is to establish and maintain a library and resource center and to publish or assist in the publication of his books, little-known articles and unpublished papers, an aspiration started by the republication of the three books of this set.

Prof. Busia published five books in his lifetime, the first his revised doctoral dissertation *The Position of The Chief in The Modern Political System of Ashanti* (1951) remains today a classic, still in print seventy years after first being published. *Urban Churches in Britain: A Question of Relevance* (1966) is remarkable for being the first sociological study by an African scholar of the British rather than the other way around as it had been for centuries. Commissioned by The World Council of Churches as a part of his World Studies of churches in mission, though it is a model in its approach, and its critique of its subject courageously honest, it remains a study of its time and place. Busia's other three books that comprise this set, though also of their time and place, concern an Africa in the throes of dynamic change and retain a relevance that make them worthy of consideration that republication will bring.

The Challenge of Africa (1962), *A Purposeful Education for Africa* (1964) and *Africa in Search of Democracy* (1967) between them are a comprehensive view into Prof. Busia's concerns published in an incredibly productive five-year period. The three books are together a wonderful reflection of Prof. Busia's work and thinking about the rapidly changing Africa of his day. His was the Africa new to independence, undergoing a thorough going soul searching on how to create the institutions that will craft new complex nations out of old equally complex societies. They have proved prescient in their articulation of the issues we are still facing to establish security and stability for ourselves and control our own natural and human resources. Busia's commitment to understanding how to pass on the heritage of the past, to cope with the present, and prepare for the future remains a constant thread throughout these works, all of which raise questions that remain with us. In dedicating his life to establishing viable liberal democracies on the African continent where each person was "his brother's keeper" Busia showed his firm conviction that liberal democracies are not an invention of ancient

Greece, but a reformulation of traditional ideas of communal caring and governance by consensus, writ large on a more complicated sense of collectivity.

Busia Foundation International is pleased to present this set *K. A. Busia on Africa* bringing these seminal works together in commemoration of the 110th anniversary of his birth and in celebration of the establishment of the Foundation. The studies are published in their entirety, but each of them with new introductions. *Where A Purposeful Education for Africa* is given another introduction by the series editor his daughter H.E. Professor Abena P.A. Busia, we are pleased to present *The Challenge of Africa* and *Africa in Search of Democracy* with new introductions which are the works of Prof. Busia himself. The on-going process of organizing the Busia archives led to the discovery of two scarcely known public presentations by Busia which now serve as wonderful introductions in his own words to the concerns of those two books. Shortly after Busia became the first African Professor at the University of Ghana in 1954, he attended the School of Advanced International Studies of the Johns Hopkins University conference on "Contemporary Africa". The address he gave as the principal speaker at the closing banquet is published here for the first time as the new introduction to *The Challenge of Africa*. This talk, given eight years before the publication of that volume, reveals how early in his career he started grappling with the issues the book covers. A decade after that dinner-time address, Busia's reputation as a fighter for democracy was firmly established. That Prof. Busia, at the time leader of Ghana's opposition in exile, was honoured to be asked, by the society for individual freedom, to speak at Runnymede on 15 June 1965 in commemoration of the seven hundred and fiftieth anniversary of the signing of the Magna Carta, makes this clear. That address now serves as the introduction to *Africa in Search of Democracy*. We hope that the republication of these works, making his own words more readily accessible will encourage the serious study of his ideas which must be the basis on which his legacy is built.

Abena P.A. Busia
Brasilia, Brazil October 2022
For Busia Foundation International
Akosua G. Busia, President

Africa in Search of Democracy

by K. A. Busia

London

Routledge and Kegan Paul

First published 1967
by Routledge and Kegan Paul Ltd
Broadway House, 68–74 Carter Lane
London E.C.4

Printed in Great Britain
by Richard Clay (The Chaucer Press), Ltd
Bungay, Suffolk

*I dedicate this book to
the Youth of Africa
to whom will fall the opportunity
and the honour of building in Africa
democratic societies wherein every man and woman
may live a life of dignity
in Freedom.*

Contents

Preface

As I reflect on the contemporary African political scene, with its bewildering upheavals and revolutions, I am frequently reminded of a passage in Plato's Protagoras (321-2):

Prometheous stole the mechanical arts and fire with them, and gave them to man. Thus man had the support of life, but political wisdom he had not ... Having no art of government, they evil entreated one another and were in process of destruction.

This book is a humble contribution to Africa's search for political wisdom whereby to avoid destruction. If any of my readers should think I have pitched my hopes for democracy in Africa too high, I can only say that I have not written as one who is a stranger to political life in Africa. I took an active part in political life in my own country in Ghana where I was leader of the Parliamentary Opposition and of the United Party which opposed the tyrannical rule of Nkrumah and his Convention People's Party. I have written this book while in voluntary exile, still continuing to oppose and expose the corruption, inefficiency and oppression of the Nkrumah regime; constantly bearing in my heart a harrowing distress at the sufferings of my former colleagues and countrymen imprisoned without trial, denied justice, ignominiously humiliated, some even maltreated to death; and painfully conscious of the reckless waste of our country's rich human and material resources.

Yet beneath all this, I discern the search for a free world in which the relations of men to one another will be brotherly and helpful rather than suspicious and savage; one in which not only the Continent of Africa but the world community will be built, in mutual respect and willing co-operation, on the common moral language which humanity shares.

This book has been made possible by the generous help I received from the African Heritage League of the United States of America and I wish to thank its Board of Directors for a memorable and fruitful association and co-operation.

K. A. B.

St. Antony's College,
Oxford

CHAPTER ONE

The Religious Heritage

In this book, I propose to examine the problems facing contemporary Africa within the context of the search for democracy; that is, for the establishment of societies which
provide the best possible conditions for individual as well as
social development within the widest measure of democratic freedom. The burning questions of nation building,
of modernization, of raising standards of living, of achieving African unity, or harmonizing race relations and world
peace, will be discussed in relation to the quest for
democracy.

We cannot fully appreciate the import of these issues, or
understand how they appear to Africans without reference
to their past, in an effort to appreciate the sentiments and
mental dispositions with which they approach their own
problems. The viewpoints and attitudes which people adopt
towards their political, economic, or social questions are influenced by their historical experiences and judgments
based ultimately on their world outlook which, conscious or
unconscious, derives from their cultural heritage. The contemporary problems of Africa must be seen in the context
of Africa's own cultural heritage.

That heritage is intensely and pervasively religious. There

are many to whom questions of religion seem irrelevant and out of place in discussing such issues as modernization and progress. It is our contention that this attitude is prejudicial to a proper appraisal of the problems of Africa as Africans see them. It is the heritage of religion which explains, for example, President Leopold Sedar Senghor's concept of African Socialism. In refutation of allegations of atheism levelled against him by his political opponents, he answered:

> The anti-federalists have accused us of being atheists, 'Marxists', and of outlawing religion. Surely this smacks of propaganda. Can we integrate Negro-African cultural values, especially religious values, into socialism? We must answer that question once and for all with an unequivocal yes.[1]

He went on to explain the fundamentally religious basis of his concept of socialism in conformity with the African religious view of life and of community.

The Government of Kenya takes a similar position where its Sessional Paper on African Socialism carries the assertion:

> Another fundamental force in African traditional life was religion which provided a strict moral code for the community. This will be a permanent feature of African Socialism.[2]

We must seek what African religion connotes in this context. President Senghor proceeded to make a comparison and a distinction which introduced a religious concept of the whole universe. He went on:

> To return to the distinction between Negro-African and collectivist European Society, I would say that the latter is an assembly of individuals. The collectivist society inevitably places the emphasis on the individual, on his original activity and his

needs. In this respect, the debate between 'to each according to his labour', and 'to each according to his needs' is significant. Negro-African society puts more stress on the group than on the individual, more on solidarity than on the activity and needs of the individual, more on the communion of persons than on their autonomy. Ours is a Community Society (*Communautaire*). This does not mean that it ignores the individual, or that collectivist society ignores solidarity; but the latter bases this solidarity on the activities of individuals, whereas the community society bases it on the general activity of the group.

Let us guard against believing that the community society ignores the person, even if we believe it neglects the individual. The individual is, in Europe, the man who distinguishes himself from the others and claims his autonomy to affirm himself in his basic originality. The member of the community society also claims his autonomy to affirm himself as a *being*. But he feels, he thinks that he can develop his potential, his originality, only in and by society, in union with all other beings in the universe: God, animal, tree, or pebble.[3]

There are several points of interest in this philosophical statement. We shall take up in the next chapter the point which deals with the concept of man in society. We shall also consider there the emphasis which African Communities place on solidarity. For the present we may note that this idea of solidarity has relevance to the growth of one-party States in Africa, though it is seldom mentioned among the many arguments often advanced to explain or justify the phenomenon. A strong predilection for a one-party state emanates from the traditional cultural emphasis on solidarity.

The point we shall take up in the present chapter is the assertion that the member of an African Society 'feels, thinks, that he can develop his potential, his originality, only in and by society, *in union with all other men, indeed with all other beings in the universe—God, animal, tree or pebble*'. This draws attention to the fact that the social, political, or economic institutions and aspirations of African peoples are closely related to their assumptions, propositions, and interpretations of the universe—of God, man, society, and nature. In the cultural heritage of Africa, this is pre-eminently within the sphere of religion, which cannot be divorced from politics, or philosophy, or economics. African religious concepts involve the whole universe.

It is recognized that there are many different communities in Africa, with different historical experiences, cultures, and religions; but from such studies as have already been done on the religious beliefs and rites of different communities, it is possible to discern common religious ideas, and assumptions about the universe held throughout Africa, and which provide a world-view that may be described as African. Religion has public and private aspects; in Africa, the private aspects deal with magic; the public aspects with community rituals and beliefs. What we attempt to do here is to select the commonly accepted ideas which give us an African world-view and interpretation of the universe.

One of the noteworthy facts which have emerged from the studies of the religious beliefs and rituals of different African communities is that they all postulate God as a Supreme Deity who created all things.[4] A maxim of the Ashanti of Ghana, one hallowed by the wisdom and tradition of the elders, is: 'No one shows a child the sky'. The 'sky' in this context symbolizes the abode of the Supreme Deity; hence the saying has been interpreted: 'No one points out the Supreme Deity to a child.' Every child knows by natural instinct that God is. The Ashanti hold that all sane human beings have a natural propensity to conceive God; and other African tribes endorse this belief. The postulate of God is universal throughout Africa; it is a concept which is handed down as part of the culture. It always has the appeal and the authority of the fathers. 'We come unto our fathers' God' is a sentiment which is echoed at the religious ceremonies of many African communities.

There are different ideas of God, but two appear to be generally held throughout Africa. One portrays God as an immanent Presence; He is everywhere. Yet this image of a pervading Presence is held alongside another which conceives God to be far away, beyond the reach of man, beyond the reach of the human mind. This is vividly conveyed in a well-known Ashanti traditional myth:

Long, long ago, God lived near to men. His abode was the sky which was then very near. There was an old woman who used to pound her fufu in a wooden mortar with a long wooden pestle. Whenever she did so, the pestle hit the abode of God which was the sky. So one day God said, 'Because of what you have been doing to me, I am taking myself far away where men cannot reach me.' So he went up and up till men could no longer reach him. Whereupon the old woman instructed her children to collect all the mortars they could find, and pile them one on top of the other. They did so, and at last they required only one mortar to add to the pile, to make it reach up to God. But they could not find another mortar. The old woman said to her children, 'take the mortar from the bottom and put it on the top'. The children accordingly removed the mortar from the bottom, but as they did so, all the other mortars rolled and fell to the ground killing many people.[5]

The myth teaches that it is not possible for man to reach up to God; it is not possible for the human mind to grasp totally the nature and dimensions of God; man may know, but not fully; he may aspire upwards, but not reach the level of the Deity, for the pervasive spirit present everywhere is also man's Creator.

Hence the polytheism of Africa; there are gods, intermediaries between man and the far-removed divine Creator, who is present in the whole universe, in everyone, and everything. God the spirit and Creator is the source of all power and energy. He is the vital Force that animates and energizes all created things; the pantheon of gods, of rivers, trees, rocks, and pebbles all derive their power from the same source. They are all parts of the universe, aspects of the one Reality.

Man also belongs to this universe, and derives his being from God. The postulate of a Creator implies the concept of man as creature, under the sovereignty of his Creator. African religious beliefs posit a realm of being beyond space and time where the individual survives. Hence man is conceived as having an immaterial part, a *soul* which does not die.

The soul-concepts of African peoples are highly elaborate. The people of Dahomey, in West Africa, for example, conceive four souls for an adult male. One is inherited from an ancestor, and is his 'guardian spirit'; another is his personal soul; a third is the small bit of the Creator that 'lives in every person's body', and the fourth is associated with a concept of destiny, bound up with the community. Every member is indissolubly bound to his community. The Dahomeans believe that a man's life cannot reach fulfilment apart from the lives of those who share that life with him. This obviously has political consequences. It is the basis of solidarity.

To take another example, the Ashanti believe that a man receives at birth two spiritual gifts from the Creator: the first is his peculiar ego, his personality, which perishes with him when he dies, and the second is his life force which, like the Dahomean conception, is that 'small bit of the Creator that lives in every person's body'. It returns to the Creator when the person dies. Everyone is thus unique and has a worth deriving from the Creator.

The postulate that individuals have souls is associated with the belief in an after-life, and with an important part of African religions. The public worship of many African tribes is directed towards the ancestors, towards the dead who are believed to survive in an after-life. There are seasonal occasions when in addition to offerings and prayers to ancestors, there are elaborate ceremonies involving rites of purification, drumming, dancing, singing, the recital of tribal history, and the reaffirmation of the values the tribe shares and cherishes. These rites, as anthropologists have observed and interpreted, give solemn and collective expression to those sentiments on which the social solidarity of the group depends. They are an expression of the unity of the tribe, and a strengthening of the sentiments which bind its members together. Again, it can be seen that this serves a political purpose as well.

Another point which may be made is that in traditional African communities, it was not possible to distinguish between religious and non-religious areas of life. All life was religious. The gods or ancestors were believed to provide good hunting or fishing grounds, or help to make fishing, farming, or hunting successful; or increase supply; or ward off evil from flocks, or crops, or man.

Even observers to whom African religions were no more

B

than systems 'of superstitions and erroneous beliefs' recognized their pervasive character.

An early account of the religious practices of an African community was given by Brodie Cruickshank in his book *Eighteen Years on the Gold Coast of Africa,* first published over one hundred years ago, in 1853. He wrote:

The character of the Gold Coast African, the nature of his government, his ideas of justice, his domestic and his social relations, his crimes and his virtues, are all more or less influenced by, and even formed upon their peculiar superstition. There is scarcely an occurrence of life into which this all-pervading element does not enter. It gives fruitfulness to marriage; it encircles the newly-born babe with its defensive charms; it preserves it from sickness by its votive offerings; it restores it to health by its bleeding sacrifices; it watches over its boyhood by its ceremonial rites; it gives strength and courage to its manhood by its warlike symbols; it tends its declining age with its consecrated potions; it smoothes its dying pillow by its delusive observances; and it purchases a requiem for its disembodied spirit by its copious libations. It fills the fisherman's net; it ripens the husbandman's corn; it gives success to the trader's adventure; it protects the traveller by sea and land; it accompanies the warrior, and shields him in battle; it stays the raging pestilence; it bends heaven to its will, and refreshes the earth with rain; it enters the heart of the liar, the thief, and the murderer, and makes the lying tongue to falter, quenches the eye of passion, withholds the covetous hand, and stays the uplifted knife, or it convicts them of their crimes, and reveals them to the world; it even casts its spells over malignant demons, and turns them for good or ill according to its pleasure.[6]

Cruickshank evinces a common prejudice when he dismisses other people's religious beliefs as 'their peculiar superstition'. What his description does correctly portray is the belief held among African communities that the supernatural powers and deities operate in every sphere and activity of life. Religion and life are inseparable, and life is not comparted into sacred and secular.

Against such a religious concept, it is not difficult to see why atheistic political doctrines have been rejected by African leaders. Senghor quotes with approval the Senegalese who on his return from Moscow said, 'The Soviet Union has succeeded in building socialism, but at the sacrifice of religion, of the soul.'[7]

This would strike an African, for in traditional African communities, politics and religion were closely associated. In many tribes, the chief was the representative of the ancestors. This enhanced his authority. He was respected as the one who linked the living and the dead. In fact, religion was linked not only with political institutions but with all social institutions. There were religious rites also associated with all the crises of life: birth, adolescence, marriage, sickness, or death; hence a religious sense of awe and reverence pervaded all life.

The religious practices of many African peoples attested that they did not only postulate God and a world of supernatural powers but also that they based their lives on that postulate. Consequently, as we contemplate the religious beliefs and practices of different African communities, we learn the role of religion in society. Their collective religious ceremonies associated with food, and harvests gave ritual recognition to the things the community valued; those connected with birth, marriage, or death taught the duties and reciprocities, and the norms of social relations within the local community or group of kinsfolk; and the joint participation in these rites gave each member a sense of belonging, and a sense of continuity.

Moreover, religion defined moral duties for the members of the group or tribe, enforced them, and provided specifically religious sanctions for them. Misfortune suffered by individuals or by the family of the tribe was often interpreted as a warning that the persons concerned should look closely into their conduct towards their kinsfolk and neighbours, or towards the supernatural powers; for misfortunes could be punishments sent because of failure to fulfil duties and obligations to kinsfolk and neighbours. Thus religion controlled conduct. It gave support to laws and customs and accepted norms of conduct, such as generosity, courtesy, honesty, or identification with one's family and kindred to promote its solidarity.

In all the religious observances of African peoples there was clear manifestation of a sense of dependence on the spiritual powers. The frequent theme of their petitions to these powers was 'We depend on you; do not let evil befall us; but give us blessing, blessing, blessing.' Their petitions may be summed up as 'Let evils go; let blessings come.' A consciousness of the inadequacy and incompleteness of man, and of his inability to cope successfully with life without supernatural aid stands out prominently in prayer and ritual.

This may be seized upon as proof of the primitiveness of the African, since there are those who contend that the difference between primitive man and civilized man is that the latter, through the competence which his technology gives him, is able to exercise control over his natural environment, and is therefore much more independent. It is true that technology increases man's control over nature, and gives him greater independence. This distinction in terms of technical competence can be validly made. As we shall see, to achieve greater technological competence is part of the quest of contemporary Africa. But there is much more to the consciousness of inadequacy and dependence manifest in African religious rites; it implies a philosophy of man which sees him as a created being dependent on his Creator. This recognition is essential to the religious life and is not altered by man's increasing technological competence.

It impels man, the created being, to seek harmony with the supernatural. However people conceive the supernatural, the impulsion to seek harmony with the Deity brings religion into practical life. Always there is a line of conduct, of things to do or forbidden, which is enjoined because it is believed that man's supreme good lies in obedience to God. This provides the ground of absolute values by which men live their lives as individuals and as members of society. Man, as implied in this philosophy, must live under the sovereignty of the supernatural.

Much of the aid to the new States of Africa tends to emphasize the provision or the achievement of material things. Africa's search is not only for things but also for spiritual values that give meaning to life. Account should be taken of the religious element of the cultures of Africa, and of the spiritual revolution taking place on the continent. This would contribute to a better understanding of its problems and aspirations.

In illustration of this, we may quote a statement of the Kenya Government:

No matter how pressing immediate problems may be, progress towards ultimate objectives will be the major consideration. In particular, political equality, social justice, and human dignity will not be sacrificed to achieve more material ends more quickly. Nor will these objectives be compromised today in the faint hope that by so doing they can be reinstated more fully in some unknown and far distant future.[8]

As is apparent from this statement, there are challenges to be faced. Traditional religious beliefs and practices face the challenge not only of universal religions like christianity and Islam but also of science and technology, and new political doctrines.

Implicit in polytheistic beliefs is the acceptance of the fact that other religious systems may be equally valid, or even more so; polytheism is a hospitable religion prepared to embrace other beliefs and practices, so long as the necessary cultural adjustments can be made to accommodate them. It makes no claim to a monopoly of truth.

Where all members of a community shared basically the same religious beliefs and participated in the same religious ceremonies, the latter were, for each member, but a part of the complex network of the social relations which constituted their way of life.

It is no longer this situation which prevails in Africa. The establishment of Islam and Christianity has made religion a potential or actual factor of tensions, and religious freedom has acquired a new significance as a democratic right. There are many States in Africa, both in the north and west, where the majority of the populations are Moslem, and where the States have a marked Islamic culture. There are others where, even though Christians are in a minority, the impact of Christianity is a major factor of social change. It becomes important and relevant when we consider that many of the leaders of contemporary Africa were educated in mission schools. The history of formal education in most of Africa is tied up with the work of Christian missionary societies. In country after country throughout the continent, Christian missionaries were the pioneers in the introduction of formal education, and still play an important role in that sphere.

The education given under missionary auspices was based on a Christian philosophy. Those who went to missionary schools and accepted Christianity were furnished with a design of living provided by the example of Jesus Christ who inspires a life of self-giving service based on love. But there were elements of Christian doctrine which questioned some of the assumptions of traditional religion about the nature of the universe.

Religion, whether traditional, Islamic, or Christian, cannot be divorced from culture. To cite the example of Christianity, African converts have been invited not only to separate themselves from their own communities by rejecting their traditional beliefs and practices but also to accept membership in different Christian Churches. This has added not only to the problems of religion, but also to the social tensions that accompany social change. It has had cultural repercussions too. Missionaries did not only carry the Christian gospel; inevitably they carried also an alien culture. They were representatives of a different culture whose way of life they could not leave behind. They took their hymns and musical forms and instruments to Africa; they built churches of Gothic architecture; they introduced their modes of worship; they imposed new ideas of family life; they taught new skills; often, missionaries were compatriots of the ruling colonial officials and governors.

Africans have thus been confronted with a choice of religions; with tensions between different codes of conduct; with encounters between different religious doctrines; with conflicts between the teaching of universal brotherhood of the universal religions of Islam and Christianity, and the fact of racial tensions between the white and black races within and outside the continent of Africa. Moreover, through books as well as press and radio, literate Africans have become acquainted with the European debate about the relation between religion and science, and about agnosticism, humanism, and atheism.

The encounter with Islam and Christianity has raised questionings and doubts about traditional religious beliefs. Nevertheless, traditional religious rites continue, and there is evidence that converts to Christianity or Islam participate in them, and resort to practices which are a part of their religious heritage, even if they imply beliefs denied by their new faiths. Indeed, independence and nationalism have been accompanied in some African States by a resurgence of traditional religious beliefs and practices. Religion remains an important element of African culture, and a potent force in contemporary life and thought, relevant to the search for modernization. Religious beliefs influence what is thought desirable, and the sort of society to which people aspire. The basic elements of African religions which are generally accepted may be briefly summarized.

This may perhaps best be done by recalling a simple Negro Spiritual which runs:

> He's got the whole world in His hands,
> He's got the whole world in His hands,
> He's got the whole world in His hands,
> He's got the whole wide world in His hands.

He's got the little tiny baby in His hands,
He's got the little tiny baby in His hands,
He's got the little tiny baby in His hands,
He's got the whole wide earth in His hands.

He's got you and me brother in His hands,
He's got you and me sister in His hands,
He's got you and me brother in His hands,
He's got the whole wide earth in His hands.

The Spiritual expresses faith in the existence of God, in His sovereignty, and in His care. The whole wide earth includes the trees, the green grass, the flowers, the rocks, mountains, the sea, the sky, the stars, animals, birds, and man. This is universally accepted in Africa.

A second element is, as we have pointed out, the consciousness of man's creatureliness and his dependence on God. This is part and parcel of African religions, all of which are Theistic. Belief in God implies the acknowledgment of his sovereignty and authority.

Tribal African religions also agree in the belief that there is an immaterial part of man which survives his existence in space and time, and that man is accountable to God for what he does with his life in this world. In the Parliament of one of the independent States of Africa, a member so frequently reminded his fellow members of their accountability to God for the way in which they discharged their responsibilities and duties that he was nicknamed Accountability. But he was appealing to a belief they all shared.

African religions support the idea that religion regulates conduct. However men conceive the Supernatural, whether as one God, or a hierarchy of gods, or of persons hallowed by death, or of consecrated objects, they give reverence, service, honour; they fall down and worship. When men see themselves to be under God, they take care to please Him; to do His will, as they apprehend it. The Supernatural provides the point of reference for their relations and standards in society. Whether the group in which they live is a homogeneous one of related kinsfolk, or a large heterogeneous one consisting of millions of people, this minimal idea of God is still applicable: men seek to make their goals and relations in society accord with the will of their God. The standards and loyalties, the obligations and reciprocities of social life in Africa are rooted in religion. Notable practical consequences flow from this concept.

The policies of neutralism, the frequent statement that European political institutions are not necessarily the best for Africa reflect the iconoclastic mood of the new Africa, rejecting the gods which other countries, whether East or West, seek to impose, whether in the form of ideologies, technology, materialism, or social and political systems. But behind Africa's search for modernization and for new political and social institutions lie an interpretation of the universe which is intensely and pervasively religious. It influences the decisions and choices Africa is making.

CHAPTER TWO

The Political Heritage

There are protagonists who have attempted to justify contemporary authoritarianism in some of the new African States by contending that it is in accord with the spirit and practice of traditional political systems; others, on the contrary, have maintained that traditional political institutions were democratic, and that it was the European Colonial Powers who destroyed democracy in Africa. This controversy calls for an examination of the traditional systems.

Traditional political systems developed in the context of communities which were families, or extensions of families, or tribes; they were kinship groups sharing a common territory, a tradition of common descent, and a common culture. The communities were characterized by poor communications, and physical isolation. The physical isolation was a consequence of the poor communications. It meant that the communities tended to be isolated from each other, and each community, turned in upon itself, fostered strong local traditions, and a strong degree of conformity. Age had both prestige and power, for it was the older people who knew and passed on to the younger the ways of the community to which they were expected to conform. The political and economic institutions which were developed were based on the intimate relationships of the members, their group consciousness, and the lack of specialization in their activities.

Wherever men live together, even if they are a group of related kinsfolk, they need to devise some way of settling claims and disputes among themselves. Political organization has its roots in the need for social order. African communities provided for the maintenance of social order through their systems of kinship. These systems played such an important role in traditional life that they have stood up to severe strains of social change, and pose difficult problems of political organization for the new States.

Sir Henry Maine's comparative study of political institutions was among the earliest of its kind. He based his study on historical data, from the history of Greece, Rome, India, Ireland, and England. In his *Lectures on the Early History of Institutions*, he offered this interesting finding:

From the moment when a tribal community settles down finally upon a definite space of land, the land begins to be the basis of society in place of kinship.... For all groups of men larger than the family, the land on which they live tends to become the bond of union between them, at the expense of kinship, ever more and more vaguely conceived.

And he illustrated this pointedly when he stated:

England was once the country which Englishmen inhabited. Englishmen are now the people who inhabit England.[1]

This aptly described a situation where the concept of citizenship had already come to be more associated with territory than with kin. This in itself reflects a historical and economic development in which the movement of populations had disrupted kinship structures, and created the need for new institutions to provide the security and the services which were formerly provided by kinsfolk.

In Africa the concept of citizenship has continued to be more closely associated with kinship than with territory. The difference is essentially one of degree of emphasis, but its institutional expression is important for political organization. The concept that 'Englishmen are now the people who inhabit England' emphasizes the idea that the territory of England is the bond of union between Englishmen. It does not preclude bonds between kinsmen; but the latter have grown weak. The secondary role has been given expression in the State and public institutions which provide the security and the services for which people once looked to their family and kinsfolk.

In Africa kinship has been, and still to a large extent is, the bond of union; this has not excluded the bond of territory, but the territory is still the place where the kinsfolk live.

Throughout Africa the isolated communities maintained high fertility rates. Everywhere there has been an emphasis on the number of children a woman bears; the more children she has, the greater the prestige for herself, her husband, and her kin. So strongly is the desirability for children enforced by custom that there are many tribes which have traditionally allowed childlessness as ground for the dissolution of a marriage. Mortality rates were high, but so were birth rates. The need to provide social security for large families accounts for the institutional emphasis on the solidarity of kinship groups. It has called for the acceptance of responsibilities and obligations for the group to a degree which gives the African concept of man a special connotation. It is a concept which sees man primarily as a member of his family; the essence of his humanity is his membership in a kinship group; it is his integration within it that makes him a human being, and gives him his status by reference to which his role within the community is defined. The whole community is kept going by the responsibilities and obligations accepted by each on the basis of his membership of the kinship group.

The Kenya Government stated in the Sessional Paper already referred to that:

Mutual social responsibility is an extension of the African family spirit to the nation as a whole, with the hope that ultimately the same spirit can be extended to ever larger areas.[2]

As will be seen, the emphasis on kinship has a bearing on the problem of nation-building in Africa. Whereas the bond of union of the tribal community has been that of kinship, a modern State consists of many different tribes. How is one to achieve 'an extension of the African family spirit to the nation as a whole'? How can one shift the emphasis from kinship groups to the State? This is one of the major problems of political organization in Africa today.

A valuable study of African political systems was made available in a volume published in 1940.[3] The book describes the political systems of eight societies widely distributed over the continent. 'We are aware,' the editors wrote, 'that not every type of political system found in Africa is represented, but we believe that all the major principles of African political organization are brought out in these essays.' Subsequent studies of political systems in different parts of the continent have provided more detail and depth of understanding, but the broad principles which emerged from the study of the eight societies described in the volume have proved to be valid and have provided a frame of reference.

It was noted that the eight political systems described in the book fell into two main categories. One group consisted of societies which had 'centralized authority, administrative machinery, and judicial institutions—in short, a government—and in which cleavages of wealth, privilege, and status correspond to the distribution of power and authority'; and a second group which consisted of 'societies which lack centralized authority, administrative machinery, and constituted judicial institutions—in short which lack government—and in which there are no sharp divisions of rank, status, or wealth'.[4] This has excited discussion as to the nature of government; we need not dilate upon the distinction here, but for our purpose, an important point to note is that in both types the lineage structure provided the framework of the political system.

Every individual is linked bilaterally through his father and mother with a number of relatives. The two sets of relationships with both one's maternal and paternal kinsmen constitute the kinship system. In African societies, one or other of the two sets of relations is emphasized above the other for status, succession to office, and inheritance to property and given institutional expression by tracing descent in a single line either through the mother (matrilineal) or father (patrilineal). A lineage consists of a group of persons who trace their descent in this unilineal way through a common ancestor or ancestress. It is one's identification with this group that gives meaning to one's existence.

It would be more concrete to illustrate some principles of political structure by taking a particular instance; and for this purpose we may choose the Ashanti of Ghana. Their system falls into the first of the two categories stated above; it is this category which is the more apposite to the problem of democratic government with which we are concerned.

The Ashanti system is matrilineal, and a lineage, which is the basic political unit, consists of members who trace their descent from a common ancestress. The community, large or small, consists of lineages that share the common territory. Where every member of the community belongs to a lineage, all can be represented through the lineage system. This is what happens in the traditional political organization: Each lineage is a political unit, and the head, chosen by the members of the lineage represents it on what becomes the governing council. It is a council of lineage heads who look after the affairs of the community as a whole.

The political organization is thus based on small social groups joining with other social groups to form a larger unit. It is based on the recognition of the sectional interests of the component groups; but it is also realized that these have to be harmonized with the wider interests of the larger unit. This principle should be noted as it has relevance to the contemporary problem of welding different tribes into a nation. The problem of building a larger political unit out of smaller units is not a new one.

A political unit has a chief, recognized as the head of the political communities. Among the Ashanti, in every political community there is a 'royal' lineage, sometimes there are several, from which the chief is chosen. Usually there are several eligible candidates who belong to the lineages

from which a chief is chosen. No one becomes a chief auto-
matically. Kin-right, that is, eligibility because one belongs
to a particular lineage, must be reinforced by election by
those to whom custom assigns that right. The principle is
one which ensures that kin-right is combined with popular
choice.

When a chief was selected and initiated into his office, he
became at once a judge, a commander-in-chief, a legislator,
and the executive and administrative head of his community. It was not many offices, but a single composite
office to which various duties and activities, rights and
obligations were attached.

An office which combined so many duties needed to be
watched, lest the holder became a tyrant. The political
system of the Ashanti provided for this contingency. It had
checks and balances. The chief's manifold duties, and the
rights and responsibilities he exercised, and his high
prestige, gave him much power; but he was given a Council to hold him in check. The chief was bound by custom to
act only with the concurrence and on the advice of his
Council. If he acted arbitrarily, and without consultation
and approval by his Council, he could be deposed. That
was one way in which the chief's powers were curbed. This
feature should also be noted. Those who elected the chief,
also had the power to depose him if he did not perform the
duties of his office satisfactorily.

There was another way in which the chief's authority
was limited, particularly in the chiefdoms spread over a
large territory. Some chiefdoms in Ashanti were very
large; and, as is well known, Ashanti became a large and
powerful confederation of chiefdoms with a king at the
head.

c

Without roads, and with the lack of means of transport and communication, the problems of administration of a large chiefdom were difficult. Apart from technical difficulties, the Ashanti were careful to prevent their chief from becoming tyrannical, and they developed a delicate balance between central authority and regional autonomy. This was an important aspect of their political structure. In matters of administration, each lineage or village managed its own affairs with a minimum of interference from the chief. That is to say, each chiefdom was run on a policy of decentralization, and there was a careful balance between the central authority of the chief on the one hand and the local autonomy of the component units of the chiefdom on the other. If the chief abused his power, his subordinate chiefs, the members of his Council, could destool him. On the other hand, if a subordinate chief or councillor tried to become too powerful, the chief could destool him. In each case, there were constitutional procedures to protect the individuals concerned, and to check arbitrariness or vindictiveness.

The best kind of democracy is the one which enables as many people as possible to share in the making of decisions, and in the actual functions of government. In the Ashanti system, the fact that each lineage, village, or part of a chiefdom managed as much of its own affairs as was consistent with the unity of the whole chiefdom enabled many to share in decision-making in local affairs; for the head of each unit was, like the chief at the centre, obliged to act only on the concurrence and with the advice of his own local council.

However autocratic a chief was permitted to appear, he really ruled by the consent of the people. There was a balance between authority on the one side, and obligation on the other. A chief or king had the power to raise taxes, or exact tribute, or ask his people to work on his farm, or even call them to take up arms to defend the chiefdom. But he had the corresponding obligation to dispense justice, or to protect the interests of his people, or ensure their welfare by certain ritual acts and observances. The ruler's subjects knew what duties they owed him; they also knew what duties he owed them, and they could exert pressure to make him discharge those duties.

There can be no true democracy where there is no free expression of opinion in public affairs or criticism of the ruling body. Any member of the community could take part in the public discussions of community affairs, or in the public hearings and 'anyone—even the most ordinary youth—will offer his opinion, or make a suggestion with an equal chance of its being heard as if it proceeded from the most experienced sage'.[5]

The members of a chief's council were, in one aspect, representatives of the people; in another sense, they and the chief constituted the government. As representatives of a section of the chiefdom, they were to protect the sectional interests of those whom they represented, and to see to it that the chief did not abuse his power; but as members of the council which had responsibility for the affairs of the whole community, they were to help to ensure the welfare of all, and to see that the people obeyed and supported the constituted authority. They shared responsibility with the chief. It is never easy to reconcile the two functions. Somebody has to keep the government or the constituted authority to the mark. None can do this better than those over whom the government rules. The Ashanti system provided opportunities for the 'commoners', those who were ruled, to express criticism, either through their lineage heads, or through a chosen leader recognized as spokesman for the commoners; through him the body of free citizens could criticize the government and express their wishes when they thought that undesirable measures were being contemplated or enforced; in the last resort, they could depose their rulers. Democracy cannot survive, unless people are able to make the government express their will; unless they have the power to choose their rulers and to change them. These principles are discernible in the indigenous political system of the Ashanti.

Though the system was designed to check any tendency towards absolute despotism, it could not prevent a ruler from failing to observe the accepted practices, and becoming a tyrant; but it could be maintained that the despotism was a violation of the system.

The pervasive influence of religion as discussed in the preceding chapter spread into the political system of the Ashanti. The most important aspect of Ashanti chieftaincy was undoubtedly the religious one. An Ashanti chief filled a sacral role. His stool, the symbol of his office, was a sacred emblem. It represented the community, their solidarity, their permanence, their continuity. The chief was the link between the living and the dead, and his highest role was when he officiated in the public religious rites which gave expression to the community values. He then acted as the representative of the community whose members are believed to include those who are alive, and those who are either dead, or are still unborn. This sacral aspect of the chief's role was a powerful sanction of his authority.

This is but a brief sketch of the political system of one of the many tribes of Africa. It cannot stand for the whole. But there are features and principles which are applicable to others. For example, there is remarkable identity with what the Kenya Government has written about the traditional system in that part of the continent:

> Political democracy in the African traditional sense provided a genuine hedge against the exercise of disproportionate political power by economic power groups. In African society a man was born politically free and equal and his voice and counsel were heard and respected regardless of the economic wealth he possessed. Even where traditional leaders appeared to have greater wealth and hold disproportionate political influence over their tribal or clan community, there were traditional checks and balances including sanctions against any possible abuse of power. In fact, traditional leaders were regarded as trustees whose influence was circumscribed both in customary law and religion. In the traditional African society, an individual needed only to be a mature member of it to participate fully and equally in political affairs.[6]

Neither authoritarianism nor the one-party State can be traced to traditional political systems like these. Arguments to justify the one-party State or authoritarianism cannot be based on the grounds of tradition. There were tribes which had hardly any institutional checks on their rulers, or where these were so ineffective as to make the system autocratic; but it is stretching the point too far to argue from this that one-party rule is a uniquely African innovation, uniformly in accord with her tradition. One-party governments can, in this twentieth century, be found in all continents, and cannot be appropriated by Africa as her own unique attribute.

In the political system of the Ashanti, one might note

three features which differ from those observed in one-party governments. As has been pointed out, the Ashanti political organization was one in which smaller political units based on the lineage amalgamated to form larger units. This posed the familiar problem of how to safeguard the sectional interests of the smaller units, and at the same time promote the common interests shared by all in the larger unit. There was always the danger that one would override the other. There was frequent temptation for those at the head of the larger unit to move towards the centralization of authority. The first feature to note about the Ashanti system is that it was based on decentralization which gave a large measure of local autonomy to the smaller units. The tendency towards centralization characteristic of one-party governments runs counter to this traditional feature.

When a council, each member of which was the representative of a lineage, met to discuss matters affecting the whole community, it had always to grapple with the problem of reconciling sectional and common interests. In order to do this, the members had to talk things over: they had to listen to all the different points of view. So strong was the value of solidarity that the chief aim of the councillors was to reach unanimity, and they talked till this was achieved. Some have singled out this feature of talking till unanimity was reached as the cardinal principle of African democracy. They have even gone farther to maintain that it is the essential mark of a democratic form of government, and that any government which has this is therefore democratic. This is going too far, for there are other important elements of a democracy. The principle is, however, noteworthy. The members of a traditional council allowed discussion, and a free and frank expression of opinions, and if there was disagreement, they spent hours, even days if necessary, to argue and exchange ideas till they reached unanimity. Those who disagreed were not denied a hearing, or locked up in prison, or branded as enemies of the community.

The councils could afford to spend hours or days of talk till they reached unanimity. They could do this because the volume of business was small, compared with what modern governments have to get through. In the new situation, local councils and legislative assemblies have wide and complex problems on which to make decisions, and there is no time to talk till unanimity is reached on every issue. So they now resort to voting, and accept and act on what the majority agree upon. But the traditional practice indicates that the minority must be heard, and with respect and not hostility. The traditions of free speech and interchange of views do not support any claim that the denial of free speech or the suppression of opposition is rooted in traditional African political systems.

The traditional systems were not perfect; imperfection is written upon all human institutions. There have been bad chiefs and councillors; there have been instances of corruption and exploitation and abuse of power; but the machinery was devised, and when it functioned well could check those in power and protect those who were ruled, and regulate behaviour for the peace and well-being of the community.

A third noteworthy feature was that there were traditional political systems which, like those of the Ashanti, allowed the people to choose their own rulers, and, as we have seen, there were alternatives to choose from. Within each kinship group there were several from whom the electors could choose. Moreover, the electors retained the right to change those whom they had chosen. This right to change their office-holders was exercised whenever the rulers failed to discharge their responsibilities and obligations in accordance with the established norms.

The hereditary element imposed a limitation on the choice of office-holders and rulers. The electors could change the office-holders, but they could replace them only by other members of the same lineage. The change of government did not call for institutions through which a minority could convert itself into a majority so as to take over the reins of power. The alternation of rulers and office-holders could only take place within the framework of the lineage system.

In the traditional political systems of Africa, the primary loyalties were centred on lineage and tribe. This was universal throughout the continent, and examples could be found from every part, north, south, central, east, or west. We may mention a few more examples. Among the Bantu, the political system was based on the kinship structures of the tribes. The chief was the head of a community held together by bonds of kinship. His office combined executive, judicial and ritual functions performed on behalf of the tribe. Among the Ngwato of Bechuanaland, the inhabitants of a village or ward generally belonged to the same tribal community and came under the leadership of a hereditary headman. Within each ward, each family, a patrilineal group, managed its own affairs under its elder. Among the Bemba, the matrilineal lineage was the basis of the political organization. Descent was traced through the mother, and membership of the lineage determined succes-

sion to different offices in the community. African political
systems were tribal structures.

There were many reasons why the tribes held together. A
tribe inhabited a common territory; its members shared a
tradition, real or fictitious, of common descent; and they
were held together by a common language and a common
culture. The environment, and the state of technology com-
pelled co-operation in the activities on which their survival
depended, whether it was food-growing, or herding cattle,
or hunting, or building a home; and the most natural unit
of organization, both for production and distribution was
the kinship group. The same kinship structure was the
basis of group religious ceremonies, especially when these
were directed towards ancestors. The tribe's common language was a bond of unity, as also of differentiation from
other tribes. From cradle to grave, every activity motivated
the individual to maintain his membership of his lineage
and tribe.

The tribal solidarity of the past invades the present. It
sets problems of political organization for the new States of
Africa. It has been a source of tensions and instability. It
has led to civil war in the Congo. Nigeria tried to contain
its tribal tensions in a federation, in an effort to achieve and
maintain democratic government. Others are attempting to
contain the tensions through the establishment of one-party
régimes, employing varying degrees of coercion and per-
suasion. In so far as traditional political structures have any
relevance to the contemporary situation, the legacy of tribalism is the most general problem it has set.

It is remarkable that this should be so, despite the fact
that the kinship system has been assailed on all sides by
economic, political, social as well as religious changes.

There are now many different ways of earning a living; people move to towns, harbours, mining and industrial areas in search of employment; cash economies, specialization, urbanization, and social differentiation have all upset the balance of dependence and the reciprocities of the family and lineage; the authority of tribal chiefs was undermined under colonial rule; and new religious doctrines and formal education threaten the beliefs which sustained the tribe. Yet in spite of these disruptive forces, the solidarity of the lineage and loyalty to the tribe continue to pose dilemmas for the creation of the modern State and its collective organs.

Some approach this problem by assuming that tribal loyalty represents a narrow loyalty which is inimical to the State. They start from the assumption that loyalty to the State is 'modern' and loyalty to the tribe is anachronistic. They seem to assume that one cannot be loyal to one's lineage or tribe, and to a larger unit at the same time. A very experienced President of an African State, one who has weathered many political storms, said calmly when asked about this: 'No President or Prime Minister in Africa today can keep his place for long without the backing of large tribes.' There are more than a hundred tribes in his State. The fact is that the tribe is not only a territorial unit but is also a unit bound together by some of the most enduring of human ties and values: shared memories and traditions, language, affectionate relationships, and a sense of security and belonging.

Some have argued that the process of nation-building requires that tribal groups should be smashed, by coercive measures, if necessary. Even in large cities of Africa, organizations based on tribal affiliations flourish and gain enthusiastic and loyal support, affording evidence that tribal cohesion is a cherished social value. It has a long tradition.

The value placed on social cohesion is an argument in favour of the establishment of the one-party State. Everyone would belong to the one party, and thus the tradition of solidarity would be carried on through the party organization. The State replaces the tribe.

The social reality is, however, more complex than that. The new African States are composed of many different tribes. A state can claim to be a common territory for all the tribes within it, but common descent, real or fictitious, cannot be maintained among tribes, some of which have a history of different origins and migrations, such as the Buale, Senufo, Guro of the Ivory Coast; the Yoruba, Hausa, Ibo of Nigeria; Ewe, Fanti, Dagomba of Ghana, to mention only a few examples from West Africa. Instead of the bond of a common culture and language, there are language and cultural differences which tend to divide rather than unite.

The social situation which is the background to the nation-building and the political experiments going on in Africa is very different from that in which the traditional political systems developed; there is a difference in scale, the areas being larger, and the populations bigger and more heterogeneous; in technology, the means of transport and communications, and the mechanisms of control are vastly more efficient; the tasks of government are more numerous. The impact of Europe has impelled social changes within which old institutions no longer function.

The most persistent legacy of traditional political systems is the value of tribal cohesion which was given expression in lineage and tribal organization. It is still a highly desired social value which the various forms of the one-party organization and other political experiments seek to preserve and express within the larger unit of the State. This aspect of the problem of political organization will be considered in the context of nation-building.

CHAPTER THREE

Colonialism

The two previous chapters indicate that there are two elements in Africa's own past which cannot be ignored in discussing the political problems of today: (1) concepts of the
universe, man, and society, expressed in religion; and
(2) the value placed on human relationships rooted in kinship groups of lineage and tribe.

Many see both the religious beliefs and tribal systems as
survivals of the primitive past which impede progress.
Among those who hold this view are Soviet writers on
African affairs. In accordance with Marxist–Leninist teaching, they maintain that religious beliefs constitute a reactionary force. In an article on Religion in the *Great Soviet
Encyclopaedia*, Yu. P. Frantsev declares:

> As an expression of the downtrodden condition and ignor-
> ance of man, religion is in its very essence anti-scientific. Re-
> ligion is the 'opium of the people'. Lenin called this dictum of
> Karl Marx the corner stone of the Marxist doctrine on religion.

Because of this attitude to religion, Soviet writers have
failed to appreciate its force in African life and thought.
But as Senghor asks:

> In the name of whom or of what, after all, does Marx dare to

affirm the dignity of man, and man's right to appropriate all the products of his labour? In the name of whom or of what does he condemn night labour, child labour, and the African slave trade unless it be in the name of a certain quality or a transcendent something beyond man? ... How can one pass from being to duty except in the name of a transcendence of religious origin?[1]

In Africa, as we have seen, religion provided sanctions for political office and duties. It was related to human conduct in all spheres of life, including political relations and roles. It is still very much alive.

Tribalism has also been seen only as a retrogressive, traditionalist force. A leading Soviet Africanist, the late Professor Ivan Potekhin, argued that tribalism was the principal obstacle to a united front in the colonies and independent States of Africa, and that tribal chiefs were the main reactionary force. Those who see it in this way advocate its forceful suppression or disintegration; but social realities show that the system cannot be dismissed in this doctrinaire way. It is a resilient system, as those who have tried to suppress it have discovered. For the majority of African communities, the kinship systems represent a secure sheet anchor in a sea of bewildering social change, and they cling to it with intense loyalty. What gives meaning and security to their lives is the network of kinship relationships within which they are sure of their rights and obligations. It is still a strong force in African politics, as appears in Chapter Seven, where we discuss it in relation to contemporary problems of political organization.

The heritage of religion and tribalism dates from the pre-colonial past; but it is colonialism which has provided the immediate background to the contemporary political problems of Africa. Colonialism is under constant fire. Some nationalists have maintained that it was colonialism which obstructed the progress of Africa. However emotionally this may be argued, it cannot be denied that in many parts of Africa there are obvious signs of material progress achieved under colonial powers. They brought administrative, commercial, and technical skills and capital; they established law and order, essential for progress; they extended commerce, built roads, railways, and harbours, opened schools, and thus laid the foundations on which the newly independent States are building.

It has also been alleged that colonialism was responsible for the 'balkanization' of Africa. This, too, is not supported by the facts of history. On the contrary, many of the present States of Africa consist of different tribal territories brought together under one administration by the colonial powers. The problem they left behind is not that of 'balkanization' but of boundaries dividing ethnic groups who thus find themselves in different States. There are boundary disputes between Ghana and the Ivory Coast, between Ghana and Togo, between Ethiopia and the Sudan, between Kenya and the Somali Republic, to mention but a few of those which have been raised during 1965, and still await settlement. These disputes point to the area in which the most serious failure of colonialism can be seen: it is evidence of failure in the area of human relations. Relatives find themselves divided by State boundaries which make them nationals of different States, though they are bound by ties of blood and language and culture.

What gave impetus to the colonization of Africa, and to the wars and rivalry of the colonial powers for the possession of territories in Africa was not primarily a concern for the welfare of the peoples of Africa as for trade and the possession of materials known or believed to exist in Africa. This was of greater force than the anti-slavery movement. The colonial powers wanted materials and set out to get them. It was things that came first, and not human beings and their welfare. Nowhere was this attitude more clearly demonstrated than in King Leopold's Congo Free State. The King's decree of 1891 required his agents to increase the production of rubber. It was quite clear that this was the main concern. His agents were to produce rubber in increasing quantity to swell his revenue. It did not seem to matter how they did it. The record of forced labour, and even of massacre committed against the Congolese between 1893 and 1904 by the King's agents in order to force the chiefs and their people to raise the quota of rubber allocated to them must rank among the darkest records of inhumanity, black even for colonial history. Whole villages were attacked and burnt down, men, women, and children were mutilated and killed, when the rubber expected from the villages was not produced. These outrages were confirmed by an official commission, and the Belgian Government took over the administration of the territory from the King. But the army and the police had a similarly bad record of coercion and ill-treatment of the Congolese. The acts of looting, burning, and rape committed by the Force Publique in the Congo in 1960 shocked the world; but it was not out of keeping with the traditions of atrocities the Congo had witnessed as a colony. There are records of outrageous ill-treatment and injustice which Africans could rake up against former colonial powers.

Colonialism in Africa was characterized by the rule of white people over black people. The whites lived in different residential quarters; they established separate clubs for themselves; the higher administrative, executive, and managerial posts were reserved for whites only: higher incomes for whites, lower for blacks. Colonial rule was an expression of the supremacy of the white races. The recent Unilateral Declaration of Independence by the white government of Rhodesia (November 1965) is only a flagrant demonstration of the most galling aspect of colonialism: the rule of a minority of whites over large populations of Africans. It is indefensibly undemocratic. It should be noted, however, that the denunciation of injustice as being undemocratic implies the advocacy of justice as an element of democratic rule.

According to Marxist–Leninist theory, imperialism is responsible for the deplorable poverty of the countries which have come under colonial rule. This has been frequently debated, one side supporting, one side stoutly defending and even maintaining (with tables and figures to support) that, on the contrary, colonial territories in Africa were a burden to imperial powers. The latter claim does not convince anyone who has been a victim of colonization, even when the figures adduced do establish that some colonies were burdens on colonial powers.

If the achievements of the colonial powers in Africa could be reduced to figures on a balance sheet, there would undoubtedly be achievements which could be entered on the credit side of the account; but on the human side, in the treatment of colonial subjects, there would be much, both of commission and omission, to be set down on the debit side. There are two aspects of the failure in human relations: one is broadly that of injustice to which we have referred, and the other is the inadequate development of

D

human resources which the granting of independence to African countries has laid bare. Its most spectacular and startling revelation has been in the Congo where there were clearly not enough trained personnel to prevent the administration from breaking down, let alone run it efficiently; but in varying degrees, the experiences of all the African countries which have been granted independence since 1951: Libya (1951), Morocco (1956), Tunisia (1956), Sudan (1956), Ghana (1957), Guinea (1958), Mauretania (1960), Togo (1960), Dahomey (1960), Senegal (1960), Mali (1960), Niger (1960), Chad (1960), Ivory Coast (1960), Nigeria (1960), Central African Republic (1960), Congo Democratic Republic (1960), Gabon (1960), the Somali Republic (1960), Malagasy Republic (1960), Cameroon (1961), Tanzania (1961), Sierra Leone (1961), Rwanda (1962), Burundi (1962), Uganda (1962), Kenya (1963), Zambia (1964), and Gambia (1965), all testify to the inadequate development of their human resources for the tasks which face them.

The concept of poverty is a complex one. It should be seen not only in terms of cash or the scarcity or underdevelopment of material resources but also in human conditions, in disease, ignorance, lack of training, and education. It should be seen in such accounts as these:

In tropical Africa, most men, women and children are habitually unwell. Many are unwell from the day of their birth to the day of their death. Many are more than unwell; they are sick of diseases, such as sleeping sickness, that are incapacitating; or of diseases that are debilitating, such as malaria and bilharziasis; or of diseases, such as bronchopneumonia and tuberculosis, that are distressing. Most of the sick are sick of more than one disease. It is nothing unusual for a person admitted to a leprosarium to be suffering from malaria, sleeping sickness, tertiary yaws, river-blindness and worm infections as well as leprosy. Left to their own devices, most of the sick have no prospect of ever being not sick. The pharmacopoeia of the medicine man is an awesome assortment of herbs, entrails, charms, and incantations. Its cures say more for the fortitude of the patient than for the skill of the practitioner.[2]

In every African country, there is the combat with disease and insanitary conditions to be waged; everywhere there is an awareness of the need for more hospitals, more doctors and nurses, more sanitary instructors, and more instruction in sanitation. Not enough was done under colonial rule. Two more illustrations may be quoted from a study undertaken in Ghana, on the eve of that country's independence:

In general the concept of good nourishment is virtually absent; it is known, of course, that life cannot be preserved without food, but the dependence of health on the quality of food is not appreciated. That food is transformed by physiological processes into body substance is too materialistic an idea to be entertained. A woman came from a village to my clinic bringing four children and asking for medicine because 'their bodies were weak'. And indeed they were: their limbs were but little sticks and they could hardly walk for fatigue. I asked what food she gave them: she replied, cocoa-yam. I inquired what else, but there was nothing else. She was wholly unable to accept, or even to consider the suggestion, that cocoa-yam was insufficient. She said they were 'only children'.[3]

And again, from the same work:

An industrious and fortunate cocoa farmer may make up to thousands of pounds in a year, but seldom is any of this spent on raising the bare standards of living. He may have a sumptuous car and driver, a wireless set, a carpeted sitting-room (seldom entered), a steel safe, a three-storey block of shops and offices in Accra or Kumasi, sons and nephews reading Law or Medicine in England or America, but he lives and eats as his fathers did—in a squalid yard where women cook on the ground and naked children swarm, crawl and eat dirt. The children may have expensive imported tricycles, but they have yaws, worms, ringworm, and deficiency diseases as freely as other children.[4]

This last excerpt shows that it is easy for a delusion of progress to be conspicuously expressed in buildings, motor cars, wireless sets, and the like, to the neglect of the human being. It is a fault which is not confined to colonial powers, but one to which African governments are also prone. This is not to excuse the colonial powers for failing to discharge their responsibilities for training their colonial subjects quickly enough or in sufficient numbers to enable them to run their States efficiently at independence, but it should be recognized that new African governments are apt to make the same mistakes through similar concentration on things instead of persons. The order of priority needs to be reversed, and human beings and their training and welfare put above things.

The deepest emotional reactions of Africans to colonialism are aroused, not by the material monuments which the colonial powers have erected but by the injustices of colonial rule, and the failures of the colonial powers to provide adequate opportunities for the development of human talent. It is in the context of race relations that Africans assess colonialism.

To illustrate this, we may follow an articulate reaction to colonialism, as it has been expressed by French-speaking

Africans in the concept of negritude. It was Aimé Cesaire, the Martinique poet and political leader who introduced the concept to express the reaction to the supremacy of the white man and his culture, as implied in the French colonial policy of assimilation. It started French-speaking African intellectuals on a search for values which could be regarded as distinctively Africa's own; values which were common to all Negroes. Negritude stood 'for the new consciousness of the Negro, for his newly gained self-confidence, and for his distinctive outlook on life, with which he distinguished himself from the non-Negro'.[5]

It is Leopold Sedar Senghor, poet, philosopher, and statesman who has developed the concept of negritude through various phases, deepening and widening the content of the concept. In its early stages, negritude expressed a militant revolt against colonialism. By 1959, this phase was already passing. In a speech delivered in France on October 2nd, 1959, Senghor said that race relations throughout the world had been characterized by 'scorn for the Negro'. Negritude was a revolt against this:

The revolt was purely negative. I confess it. The Negro students of whom I was one in the years 1930-4 were negativists. I confess we were racists. We were delirious in our negritude. No dialogue was then possible with Europe.

Some critics of the concept of negritude do not appear to have observed the development of the concept since this early phase. Senghor did join in the search to discover a quality common to all Negroes. He first expressed it as 'heightened sensibility and strong emotional quality. Emotion is Negro.' He explained that the attempt to rediscover the past was 'not simply a question of resuscitating the past, or trying to live *dans le musée Negro-Africain*; but of animating the world of today with the values of the African past'. The link between the quest and the colonial policy of France was shown by President Senghor when in a speech delivered at Oxford in October 1961 he said:

> Paradoxically, it was the French who first forced us to seek its essence (i.e. of Negritude) and who then shewed us where it lay when they enforced their policy of assimilation and thus deepened our despair. We set out on a fervent quest for the 'holy grail'—our collective soul.

As he stated on that occasion, the concept of negritude had widened in scope to include 'the whole complex of civilized values—cultural, economic, social, and political, which characterize the black peoples, or more precisely the Negro-African world'. Since Negroes belong to different nationalities and cultures, this is no easy thing to discover. What are the common values? According to Senghor, they are 'the sense of communion, the gift of myth making, the gift of rhythm—such are the essential elements of Negritude which you will find indelibly stamped on all the works and activities of the black man'.

The reaction to colonialism had a positive side to it in the desire to uplift the black man who had been the object of scorn. His dignity was to be asserted. This was the reason for delving into the past to discover values that belonged distinctively to the Negro African. At a Conference held at Abidjan in April 1961 on the subject of 'The Contribution of Religion to the Expression of the African Personality', Bernard Dadie of the Ivory Coast explained this aspect of negritude:

> The desire to *be* gave birth to the theory of Negritude: this

Negritude which has caused so much ink to flow was stirred in us by the frustration of being deprived in the course of history of the joy of creating and being regarded at our real value. Negritude is nothing but our humble and tenacious ambition to rehabilitate the victims and to demonstrate to the world what has been specifically denied up to this time: the dignity of the black race.

It is thus in the context of race relations that negritude is to be understood. Colonialism, white domination over black, and apartheid have one thing in common; they are all seen as an affront to the dignity of the black man. The sentiment is shared alike by all colonial subjects whether they have come under British, French, Belgian, Portuguese, or Spanish rule.

But the concept of negritude has, in the hands of Senghor, passed beyond its militant anti-European and racist stage to a mellower tone where it shows an awareness of a wider brotherhood of man. Said President Senghor at Oxford:

If we are justified in fostering the values of Negritude, and arousing the energy slumbering within us, it must be in order to pour them into the mainstream of cultural miscegenation; they must flow towards the meeting point of all humanity; they must be our contribution to the civilization of the universal.

This wider concept acknowledges that some good did come out of colonization.

Seen within this prospect of the civilization of the universal, the colonial policies of Great Britain and France have proved successful complements of each other and black Africa has benefited. The policies of Great Britain tended to reinforce the traditional native civilization. As for France's policy, although we have often reviled it in the past, it too ended with a credit balance through forcing us actively to assimilate European civilization. This fertilized our sense of Negritude. Today our Negritude no longer expresses itself in opposition to European values, but as a complement to them.

Those who still see African politics in terms of racism, and are constantly declaiming against colonialism and neo-colonialism disapprove of this development of negritude. Senghor has stretched the concept even wider. It has now become a philosophy of humanism; but a humanism that has room for God. In his Oxford speech of 1961, he asserted :

Our revised Negritude is humanistic. I repeat it welcomes the complementary values of Europe and the white men, and indeed of all other races and Continents. But it welcomes them in order to fertilize and reinvigorate its own values, which it then offers for the construction of a civilization which shall embrace all mankind. The neo-humanism of the twentieth century stands at the point where the paths of all nations, races, and Continents cross, where the four winds of the spirit blow.

This widening of the concept has affected Senghor's appraisal of the results of colonialism. To those who smart under a continuing sense of injustice and nurse gnawing injuries, his conclusions are unpalatable.

Let us [he admonishes] stop denouncing colonialism and Europe and attributing all our ills to them. Besides being not entirely fair, this is a negative approach, revealing our inferiority complex, the very complex the colonizer inoculated in us and whose accomplices we thereby are secretly becoming. It is too easy an alibi for our own laziness, for our selfishness as intellectuals, for our failures. It would be more positive for us and our people to analyse the colonial fact objectively, while psycho-analysing our resentment.

Senghor's own objective analysis is that

examined in historical perspective colonization will appear at
first glance as a general fact of history. Races, peoples, nations,
and civilizations have always been in conflict. To be sure, con-
querors sow ruin in their wake, but they also sow ideas and
techniques that germinate and blossom into new harvests.

In the hands of its leading exponent, the concept of negritude has developed from a racist, militant reaction to
colonialism to a wide humanism and generous assessment
which now sees colonialism in terms of co-operation and
involvement rather than condemnation and unyielding
opposition.

The Soviet view of negritude is different. Potekhin con-
cluded an article in *Kommunist* (No. 1, 1964, pp. 104–13)[6]
by saying that negritude

began with anti-racialism and with the condemnation of the
colonial policy of French imperialism, but ended in alliance
with it. The supporters of 'negritude' were directed towards
this unnatural alliance with the oppressors, above all, by their
denial of the alliance of the oppressed nations of Africa with the
European proletariat.

What Potekhin found ideologically unacceptable was
that the supporters of negritude 'admit that colonialism is
an evil, but they proclaim "we shall make an end of re-
proaches, and we shall be more attentive to the contribution
than to the damage" '. Yet that attitude is not only more
magnanimous, it is also more realistic. The former colonial
powers are important members of the world community to
which Africa seeks entry on equal terms.

We may ask what contribution colonialism has made to
the development of democratic régimes in Africa. It is

easier to see the contributions which could have been made but were not made, since these are shown in the weaknesses and needs of the States which have gained independence. In all of them, we find that neither agricultural nor industrial development was at a stage where the standards of living of the bulk of the populations were much above subsistence levels. All the countries are classified as poor and under-developed. In all of them the raising of the standards of living is a major task which must have priority. That situa-tion also discloses the inadequate development of human resources to which we have referred. There are not enough men with the necessary skills. Education has not been re-garded as an essential investment for development. The newly independent States have been faced with severe shortage of manpower for the civil and defence services and their development projects. In some this has made in-dependence more formal than real.

All this is apt to diminish the importance of the contri-bution that colonial powers have made. Works[8] dealing with the early history of colonial administration give a picture of what has been done. In the Gold Coast, for example, personnel was brought from Sierra Leone and the West Indies during the nineteenth century to fill posts in the clerical and administrative services, and in the police and military forces, because no literate persons were avail-able in the country, and malaria took a heavy toll of Euro-peans. Then schools were opened, and people were trained first for junior posts, and later for more senior ones. By the time of independence in 1957, there were Africans in all branches and at all levels of the Civil Service, headed by an African. An administrative framework had been provided. In all the colonies, there are accounts of the establishment of law and order, which was necessary for the development of trade and commerce. The cities of Africa and the big commercial centres are symbols of the development of commerce and industry. The contribution of colonialism was the provision of a stable political framework within which development could take place.

This contribution can be frankly acknowledged, as the supporters of negritude have done. But what contribution was made towards the development of democratic régimes? The colonial régimes were themselves authoritarian and paternalistic. They operated institutions which made it possible for a minority of whites to rule large African populations.

The administrative system in the rural areas, whether under the French or the British did not allow local participation in decision making. The British, under the system of indirect rule, worked through traditional institutions, but in the process changed their character. The chiefs were placed in a position where they were partly representatives of their people, and partly agents of the imperial power, and the checks and balances of the indigenous systems could no longer operate democratically. They were undermined by the control of the administering power.

The French followed a policy which destroyed the existing tribal systems. They divided each colony into districts and cantons, often without regard to ethnic ties, and appointed so-called chiefs who were agents of the government. Where chiefs belonging to old 'royal' lineages were used, they acted more as agents of the colonial régime than in their hereditary roles. So in both British and French territories, the chiefs became identified as 'stooges' of the colonial government. In no territory in Africa did the colonial régimes establish local self-governing institutions. Local administration was under the control of appointed agents.

British policy followed a series of constitutional changes which led to the granting of 'internal self-government' as the last stage before independence. This was marked by elections to a Legislative Assembly, and parliamentary government by a Cabinet of ministers, usually with the ministerial posts of Justice, Finance, and Defence held by Colonial Administrators. The leader of the party that won the elections became the Leader of Government Business. The party in power was thus given experience and was helped in many ways. The new ministers had expert help from experienced civil servants and from their ministerial colleagues; they had the prestige and patronage of office for building up and strengthening their party. They could use official positions and appurtenances for party purposes.

The British teach that an opposition is an essential part of the parliamentary democratic system; yet their policy for helping the institution of the parliamentary system at this final stage never included any official help to the opposition. Three British administrators sat on the Front Bench with the government; and an array of experienced civil servants sat behind the government benches, always ready to send notes and answers to the members of the government to save them from being shown up by the opposition, while members of the opposition had to fend for themselves, without any help. Handicapped in many ways, held up to the country by the propaganda of their opponents in government as 'enemies of the people', and with the civil servants and administrators of the colonial régime weighted against them, it is no surprise that the opposition was often crushed. Yet explanations of opposition failures and weaknesses do not take account of the fact that the policy of the colonial government included help for the party that won elections, and no help for the party that formed 'Her Majesty's Loyal Opposition'. Neither at the centre nor at the local level can it be said that strong foundations for democratic rule were laid. The shoot was very tender, easy to smother under the authoritarian framework that is bequeathed at independence.

Under the French system, some of those who later led independence movements in the colonies, or headed the governments, such as President Houphouet-Boigny of the Ivory Coast, or President Senghor of Senegal, received experience in official posts in France. But the French colonies that have received independence since 1960 have done so at a time when, as French political scientists have themselves pointed out, France has been moving towards a type of monarchical republic, in the Fifth Republic under General de Gaulle, with a dominant executive and a weak, almost powerless parliament. This evolution has set an example not markedly different in effect from the one-party constitutions which have been adopted in the French-speaking States.

The more remarkable contribution to democratic rule is provided by ideas and techniques: ideas of justice, of impartial and independent courts; ideas of freedom of speech, discussion, worship, and travel; ideas of the rule of law, and the idea of social justice which is only a sham without these essential freedoms and civil liberties. To the contribution of ideas must be added the techniques of voting, of administration, or running modern enterprises, and a modern State.

For administration, language is necessary, and since African States are divided by many languages, the legacy of French or English which brings different tribes into conversation with one another within their common State, and brings Africans into conversation with the world outside, must be reckoned one of the contributions to democratic rule.

It cannot be said of colonial régimes that they were shining examples of democracy; nor can it be justly claimed that the newly independent States inherited from them democratic institutions suited to their condition. What the colonial powers have left is a foundation of democratic ideas and techniques which can help a country whose leaders wish to establish a democratic form of government; they have also left institutional frameworks of centralized administration with a tendency towards authoritarianism which can be, and in some States have indeed already been adapted to that end.

CHAPTER FOUR

Communist Prescriptions
for Democracy

Among the strong influences on contemporary African thought and policies on the subjects of development and democracy are those exerted by Communism, as propagated by the Soviet Union and China. We may therefore in this chapter briefly summarize what the two countries have been imparting to Africa. To some readers this may all be familiar, but it is a necessary link in the development of our subject, as is shown in the subsequent chapters where we discuss African concepts of Socialism and Democracy.

Soviet leaders and writers claim that the Bolshevik Revolution of 1917 sparked off a liberation movement which has spread to Africa. They feel proud of the contribution they have thus made to the birth of independent States in Africa. The Soviet report on the Second Afro-Asian Solidarity Conference which was held in Conakry in April 1960 began with the words: 'The Soviet people is justly proud that the Great October Socialist revolution opened a new era of the development of mankind, an era of justice, an era of true humanity.' One Soviet author has claimed that the revolution was the first example of a rising which ended in the genuine victory of the popular masses, among whom were the peoples of the Tsarist colonies. This reference to Tsarist colonies is to underscore the fact that the revolution began the battle for colonial freedom. Another author has stated more specifically that the 'crisis of the colonial system in Africa began under the influence of the Great October Socialist Revolution'. Its link with Africa has been made even closer by the assertion that it 'undermined the racial myth of the superiority of the white man'.[1] Since colonialism in Africa has been characterized by the domination of whites over blacks, the reference to 'the racial myth' makes the African colonial struggle very much a part of the earlier October revolution.

The same assertion was made in a statement issued at a meeting of representatives of eighty-one Communist and Workers' Parties held in Moscow in November 1960. According to the statement, the Russian revolution 'drew the colonial peoples into the current of the world-wide revolutionary movement'. The victory which the Soviet Union achieved during the Second World War, the establishment of Peoples' Democracies in Europe and Asia, the successful socialist revolution in China, were all cited in support of this contention. The socialist system, it was said, had become a 'reliable shield' for the newly independent countries; and Communists, the statement claimed, 'have always recognized the progressive, revolutionary significance of national liberation wars, and are the most active champions of national independence'.[2]

The Soviet Union comes to Africa as a friendly country which did not take part in the colonization of Africa; on the contrary, she claims to have started the liberation movement, and also to be in sympathy with African aspirations. As evidence of this, we may refer to the official message which Prime Minister Kruschev sent to the Addis Ababa Conference of African States in May 1963. In response to the resolutions passed at the Conference, the Soviet leader sent a message supporting general and complete disarmament, the making of Africa into a nuclear-free zone, the removal of foreign troops and bases from the continent, the boycotting of States guilty of racial discrimination or colonialism, and the expansion of trade. These were all causes in which the Soviet Union avowed common accord with the African States.

But what does the Soviet Union offer to Africa in her quest for democracy? By the Soviet Union's own concept of democracy, no African State is yet fully democratic, or indeed truly independent; but if any State accepts the Soviet concept, then the Soviet Union has much guidance and help to offer. The Soviet concept of democracy is embodied in its socialist ideology. We may refer to a few instances. The Communist and Workers' Parties meeting in Moscow in November 1960 discussed the status of certain newly independent States, in the context of their ideology. None of those States could be accepted as fully democratic, but some were deemed to have established a status described as 'national democracy' which was defined as a State which

constantly upholds its political and economic independence; fights against imperialist and military blocs and bases, and against new forms of colonialism; rejects dictatorial and despotic forms of government; ensures democratic rights and freedoms for its people, and their participation in agrarian reforms, and in shaping government policy.

According to the statement issued by the meeting, 'national democratic tasks' which fall in line with the above definition of 'national democracy' are

E

the consolidation of political independence, agrarian reforms, elimination of the survivals of feudalism, the liquidation of imperial economic domination, the creation of a national industry, improvement of the living standard, the democratization of social life, the pursuance of an independent and peaceful foreign policy, and the development of economic and cultural co-operation with the socialist and other friendly countries.[3]

These tasks add up to the familiar Communist ideology to which the statement gives a clue when it says that in the effort to establish a 'national democracy' the

people begin to see that the best way to abolish age-long backwardness and improve their living standard is that of non-capitalist development. Only thus can the people free themselves from exploitation, poverty and hunger. The working class and the broad peasant masses will play the leading part in solving the basic problem.

The status of 'national democracy' as formulated by the meeting was further discussed in several articles in the Soviet Union. We may refer to two of them, for the light they throw on the Soviet concept of democracy. Academician Ye Zhukov discussed the concept of 'national democracies' in an article in *Pravda*.[4] His main conclusion was that whatever course a country liberated from colonialism decided to follow, historical experience showed that only the non-capitalist road of development would ensure the solution of social problems, and the raising of the living standard of the masses.

In a booklet on 'The National Liberation Movement in Africa'[5] another Soviet author, A. M. Sivolobov, discussed what, in the Soviet sense, was the 'democratic content' of African nationalism. His view was that there were two tendencies in the African independence movement. One was

the tendency of certain national bourgeois parties to acquiesce in mere formal independence, without due regard for the fundamental interests of their people; the other was the tendency of 'progressive' national leaders to aim at making independence a reality by putting their countries' natural resources at the service of their peoples.

Those in the first category, we are told, 'try to remain in the British Commonwealth or the French Community'. Examples of the second category were given as Guinea, Mali, and Ghana, although Ghana is a member of the Commonwealth.

Sivolobov emphasized the importance of the working class in the struggle for independence and economic growth; for in order to fulfil Communist doctrine, 'democratic' nationalism must have class roots. 'Democracy must assert the rights of the masses.' Soviet elucidations invariably arrive at the same conclusion, namely, that of the Soviet ideology of scientific socialism.

The recurrent theme of Soviet writers is that political independence for Africans means little unless they free themselves from the capitalist economies of the West and cooperate with the socialist camp. In an article in *Aiya I Afrika Segondnya*,[6] V. I. Povlov explained that co-operation with Socialist States 'promotes the emergence of the most democratic, anti-imperialist facets of the public sector'. The public sector, he said, may develop in one of two directions: it may take the democratic course of economic independence 'through industrialization, and elimination of feudal anachronisms', or the course of 'subjection to bourgeois land-owning reactionaries'. It will take the first course if the working class and peasantry rally to its support by forming 'a national democratic front'. So again the importance of the role of the working class is emphasized. This is all in accordance with Marxist–Leninist doctrine. National bourgeois governments only embark on the democratic road when they build economic systems which become 'the property of a working-class régime'. The way for a former colony to become truly independent and free is to rid itself of all Western influence and accept Communism. This, in short, is the Soviet concept of democracy.

The newly independent States of Africa are therefore not yet democratic. They have all, in the Soviet view, been under the ideological influence of capitalist Europe and America, and are already capitalist States in which capitalist bourgeoisie have begun to exploit the labour of others. African society in these States, as seen by the Soviets, consists of small producers, private property owners, and petty bourgeoisie.[7]

For example, V. Kudryavtsev has attacked the French 'ideological legacy' in the French-speaking African countries, deploring the fact that many of the African intelligentsia were educated in Paris and that 'some important present-day leaders even occupied ministerial posts' in France.[8] This is a gibe at President Houphouet-Boigny of the Ivory Coast under whose leadership in 1950–1, the first effective political organization in French-speaking Africa, the Rassemblement Démocratique Africain (RDA) broke with the French Communists. The RDA which was formed in 1946 had branches in all the French-speaking colonies, but it came under the controlling influence of French Communists. It now survives in the Regional parties of French-speaking Africa. Kudryavtsev also stated that in the majority of the former French colonies in Africa, the local upper class which had come to power considered that the achievement of State independence was 'the consummation of the national liberation movement' whereas the situation was one in which 'de jure independence disguises the almost unaltered domination of French monopolies in the economy of these African countries'. In the Soviet view, true freedom and independence can only be assured by 'scientific socialism'.

Owing to the control which 'Capitalist Colonialists' exercised over African countries, as Professor Potekhin once told the writer, it is only after independence that opportunities open for the penetration of socialist ideology. He was then planning to visit Nigeria soon after it became independent.

As we shall see in the next chapter, African leaders avow various shades of Socialism, none of which are accepted by Soviet authorities as being of the genuine brand. For example, L. Pribytkovskiy and L. Fridman in a joint article entitled: 'The Choice before Nigeria',[9] scathingly attacked all the three major parties of Nigeria, the Action Group (AG), the National Convention of Nigerian Citizens (NCNC), and the Northern People's Congress (NPC) when a Nigerian Daily, the *West African Pilot*,[10] published that 'all the three parties accepted Socialism as their guiding principle'. On this, the authors commented:

Statements of this kind need to be at least more precisely formulated. For instance, the NPC leaders, who include the ruling feudal circles and bourgeois elements in the North, have never expressed themselves in favour of socialism. It would indeed be strange to expect any acknowledgment of socialism as a guiding principle by emirs and sultans who still keep firm hold of the prerogatives of spiritual and temporal power over millions of Nigerians. The other two parties, the NCNC and the AG, have both in fact declared their adherence to socialist ideals and their desire to create a socialist-type society. However, the leaders of both these parties have their own ideas about socialism and give their own interpretation of basic social and economic phenomena—one which is very different from the scientific concept of socialism.

They castigated the 'democratic socialism' of the Action Group as a form of mixed economy which combined both private and State capitalist sectors, and, moreover, included a sector controlled by foreign monopoly capital. 'It is therefore not scientific socialism.'

Similarly, the 'pragmatic socialism' of the NCNC was described as 'an extremely ill-defined concept which has nothing in common with scientific socialism'.

The two authors conclude with the familiar doctrine that only by relying on the working class as the most consistent revolutionary force in society can fundamental social problems be solved. The leaders of the new States 'will either understand this or they will be succeeded by other people who will have a better understanding of the demands put by life'.

In an article written a month before,[11] Potekhin had, in 'A Reply To My Opponents', attempted to answer protagonists of 'African Socialism'. He pointed out that according to scientific socialism it was essential to eliminate private ownership of the means of production, and to make them public property, and dismissed as 'utopia' the 'idea entertained by some supporters of "African Socialism" that private enterprises could be retained under socialism, and that exploitation could be eliminated under private ownership'. That was only a false idea to preserve capitalism. In answer to those who maintained that pre-colonial African society was already socialist, Potekhin replied:

Before the colonizers came, many African peoples were living in a primitive communal society, knowing neither exploitation nor the division of society into classes. If equality existed among those people, it was equality of poverty, whereas a socialist society is a society of abundance.

In another article written a year later in *Kommunist*, on 'Negritude, Pan-Africanism, and African Socialism',[12] Potekhin examined African socialism again; his remarks contained an outburst which is an excellent illustration of how Communist propaganda and scholarly works are often inseparably interlocked:

There is no single concept of African socialism; it has many variations. An attentive study of all these variations shows that in some cases it is the result of a delusion of people who are sincerely striving for socialism, while in others it is the reflection of the interests of the growing African national bourgeoisie, which reckons on using certain socialist methods (economic planning, the creation of a state sector in the economy, and other things) to do away with the economic backwardness of the country without damaging its own interests. But, no matter how theoreticians in Africa and abroad interpret the concept of 'African socialism', the popular masses of the African Continent see in it the idea of a categorical rejection of the capitalist path of development, and the idea of ridding themselves, not only of imperialist exploitation but also of the exploitation of man by man, that is, the idea of genuine scientific socialism. The workers attach their hopes for a better life to the idea of social-ism, that socialism which has already led a third of mankind on to the road of happiness, freedom and justice, and in this consists the most important victory of our epoch. There is no doubt that the masses will find the right forms for the transition to socialism, taking into account the concrete peculiarities of African countries.

Some leaders of young African States maintain that Marxism is inapplicable in African countries, because in them there are no classes of the proletariat and the bourgeoisie. But Marxism is, specifically, a doctrine of the most general laws of development of any society, including the pre-capitalist. It embraces the concept of a non-capitalist course, that is, the development which, by-passing the capitalist stage, may lead to socialism, in precisely those countries where bourgeoisie and proletariat have not been able to form. The idea of non-capitalist development is finding wide recognition in Africa; this is one more confirmation of the obvious truth that Marxism is applicable to all continents and countries, including Africa.

It may be asked on what data Professor Potekhin based the findings which enabled him to speak with such authority on behalf of the 'popular masses of the African Continent'; and indeed who the 'popular masses' are. Judging from his own writings, he did not find the workers, or the trade unions, or the peasants of Africa ready to play the role of a 'revolutionary vanguard' of scientific socialism. The workers as a whole are said to lack organization and class consciousness, and the thousands of migrant workers on mines and farms throughout Africa are 'the most backward and least conscious part of the working class'. As for the trade unions, Professor Potekhin found 'the almost complete illiteracy of the workers' to be a serious obstacle. The peasants were even less suitable. He described them as 'an uncompacted, atomized mass of small producers, illiterate, and politically extremely backward'. The Soviet Party Programme of 1961 condemned as 'petty bourgeois illusion' a socialism which excluded class struggle. It is therefore difficult to see how the 'popular masses' who lack class consciousness fit into the picture he has painted.

The social realities of Africa pose baffling questions for Soviet theoreticians, and some of the answers they have offered have been contradictory. We have one example in the paragraphs we have just quoted. In orthodox Marxism, the capitalist stage is presented as being an essential one for the progression to socialism, since the advance is a dialectical process of the class struggle. Here, however, Potekhin states a new version of the theory which says that 'the pre-capitalist stage by-passing the capitalist stage may lead to socialism', thus making Marxism 'applicable to all countries, including Africa'. This version is meant to counter the argument that Africa does not conform to the image of a class society, and to convince the new African States that though they can 'leap' from the pre-capitalist stage to socialism, Marxist–Leninist theory provides for such a situation. Potekhin claims that in the Soviet Union, the peoples of Central Asia and of the Mongolian Peoples' Republic have proceeded direct to socialism from a primitive communal structure. But what happens to the dialectic of the class struggle which the party programme, conforming to the orthodox doctrine, has pronounced that it is 'a petty bourgeois illusion' to consider that it can be excluded from socialism? In *Africa Looks Ahead*, Potekhin gives the answer that Marx did not consider the capitalist stage of development inevitable for all peoples and all countries, and that Lenin declared that, with the aid of the proletariat of the advanced countries, backward countries could advance to Communism 'by-passing the capitalist stage of development'.

Despite this defence of the new theory, Soviet Africanists have not abandoned the orthodox position. In *Africa Looks Ahead*, Potekhin himself maintains that African society has class differentiation, and that Marxist–Leninist theory is as applicable there as anywhere else. The conclusions of three studies of African societies published in *Sovetskaya Etnografiya* in 1960–1,[13] support Potekhin's view. M. I Braginskiy in *Social Advances in Tropical Africa* finds a rapid dissolution of tribal relations after the Second World War of 1939–45, and the formation of working class, national bourgeoisie, and intelligentsia, and hence a capitalist society. V. Ya Katsman in an article on 'The Growth of Property Differentiation among the African Peasantry of Tanganyika after the Second World War', finds the introduction of cash and commodity relations to have resulted in property differentiation, and the emergence of the first stages of capitalist relations. The third study on 'The Place and Role of the Traditional Authorities of African Societies' goes farther back in time. In that study, A. S. Orlova finds that the medieval states of the Western Sudan and the Guinea Coast were already class societies before Europeans appeared there in the fifteenth century. Although the tribal systems were tenacious, undeniable elements of a class society appeared in property inequality, domestic slavery, and extensive barter trade, and powerful hereditary chiefs.

So in spite of the new formulation of theory to cover the direct advance to socialism from a pre-capitalist stage, all the studies affirm that, as a matter of fact, African societies have had or are developing capitalist relations in accordance with orthodox Marxist–Leninist theory.

But the contradictions on African issues cannot be hidden. They have become more obvious from the conflict between the Soviet Union and China. At the same time that some Soviet theoreticians were telling the new States of Africa that it was possible for them to jump the capitalist stage, and advance to socialism from a pre-capitalist stage, others were upbraiding the Chinese Communists for holding the view that it was possible to take a short cut to Communism. The Chinese were to understand that the laws of history could not change, and that, in the words of Eugene Zhukov, 'it is impossible to jump over a certain historical stage'.

The contradictions also appear, for example, in the interpretation each of the two countries gives to 'co-existence' in their diplomacy and policy in Africa. As part of their faith in the ultimate victory of Communism all over the world, both countries hope that Africa will one day be under Communist control; as an immediate objective, both countries hope at least to deprive the 'imperialist' countries of the West of strategic bases, and of political and economic advantages in Africa. How is co-existence to be interpreted in the African situation? The meeting of the eighty-one Communist and Workers' Parties held in Moscow in 1960 agreed that co-existence between States was a form of class struggle between socialism and capitalism. It did not mean a reconciliation between socialist and bourgeois ideologies; on the contrary, it implied an intensification of the struggle. In Africa, this must include the struggle against the imperialism of the West.

Both countries agree that the world-wide victory of Communism can come about by peaceful transition or by revolution, and that from the Marxist–Leninist point of view it would be in the interest of the proletariat to take advantage of an opportunity of peaceful transition to socialism. But, paradoxically, China's view is that no policy can be built on peaceful transition, for there is not a single example in history of a peaceful transition from capitalism to socialism. The policy for world Communism must be built on revolutionary struggle.

The Soviet Union, on the other hand, advocates a policy of 'peaceful co-existence'. This does not rule out revolution, but it apparently expresses preference for advancing the cause of Communism by negotiation, wherever possible. Consequently, the Soviet Union emphasizes support for social and economic progress in Africa, in contrast to China's appeal for violent revolution.

The Soviet Afro-Asian Committee distributed a statement at the meeting of the Executive Committee of the Afro-Asian Peoples' Solidarity Conference held in Nicosia in September 1963 in which it was stated that the Soviet policy of peaceful co-existence referred only to inter-State relations, and not to relations between oppressed and oppressors. It would be right to use revolutionary methods in the colonial struggle. The difference between the Soviet Union and China appears to be one of emphasis, but it is fundamental and contradictory. It marks the ideological war between the two Communist countries which has been carried into Africa.

At the Fourth Peoples' Solidarity Conference held in Winneba, Ghana, in May 1965, the Chinese were able to get the Conference to condemn 'peaceful co-existence' as a completely unsuitable way of gaining progress for national liberation movements. The Chinese put forward the view that whoever negotiated with the imperialists was supporting 'peaceful co-existence', and whoever did that was an ally of imperialism. Instead of disarming, the new States were urged to strengthen their defences and build up a revolutionary organization. The question is whether the Communist victory, assumed as inevitable, is to come by armed struggle or by negotiation. Is the Soviet advocacy of negotiation only a ruse? Which side is correctly interpreting Marxist–Leninist doctrine? Each side claims that the other is departing from the true path. The ideological dispute is part of a battle between the two countries for hegemony. Their policies aim at the eventual triumph of Communism in Africa, and indeed in the world; but is it to be under the leadership of the Soviet Union or China?

Since their rivalry came into the open in the autumn of 1959, the Soviet Union and China have followed different policies in Africa, and the Communist case has been clouded by their rival claims and propaganda and inherent contradictions. They both teach that in order to achieve full independence and democracy, the African countries must attain economic independence, and that the only way to do this is to follow the non-capitalist path by developing economic and cultural ties with Communist countries. The Soviet Union points to its own achievements, and sets itself up as the model to be followed; while China maintains that it is the Chinese example which is more appropriate to the condition of the developing countries of Africa, and that the Russian model calls for higher levels of technology than Africa possesses at present.

Industrial development and modernization call for big capital which the new African States do not possess. They therefore require capital investments from outside. But Soviet propaganda warns them against receiving capital from the Western European countries or America. It is argued that they are imperialists who are willing to help only because they wish to exploit Africa's need for capital in order to impose a more dangerous form of domination—neo-colonialism.

Thus Nigerians were told by Soviet experts that Western aid was a variant of neo-colonialism which threatened Nigeria's economic emancipation. It was to the socialist system and the socialist countries that they should look for aid which would ensure freedom. The Soviet construction of the metallurgical works at Blulai in India and the Aswan High Dam in the U.A.R. were cited as examples of disinterested Soviet aid.

Soviet aid was defended on the grounds that it is only given in the State sector, and a State-controlled economy would stimulate the growth of the working class, and restrict that of the bourgeoisie. It therefore helped development along the non-capitalist path. But the theoreticians are not agreed on this. Potekhin says in *Africa Looks Ahead*, that 'it is a delusion to conclude that enterprises which belong to the State are thereby the possession of the people as a whole, that is to say socialist property'. A bourgeois State 'always and unfailingly defends the interests of only one class, the capitalists, to the detriment of the interests of the workers; enterprises which belong to it therefore are the collective property of the capitalist class'.[14] So State capitalism is another point of ideological dispute. Does it contribute to the development of Communism (and therefore by Communist definition to full independence and democracy), or is its contribution mainly to the common struggle against imperialism?

Whatever the theoretical answer, the Soviet Government has developed diplomatic and economic contacts with the

States of Africa on the basis of its policy of peaceful co-existence. The plan seems to be to draw a State into the Soviet-dominated industrial market through aid and trade pacts; it is expected that through this relation, experts or properly trained Communists would come to occupy key points in the State capitalist economy, and as the State capitalist sector grows, the economic changes and the attendant social changes would turn the State into a social-ist state. Industrialization and modernization therefore pre-cede the social revolution, which in such a case would be achieved without violence.

But the Chinese approach puts the social revolution first. In an address given at the opening session of a Conference of the World Federation of Free Trade Unions (WFTU) in Peking in November 1949, Liu Shao-Chi stated that

the course followed by the Chinese people in defeating imperial-ism and its lackeys, and in founding the People's Republic of China is the course that should be followed by the people of the various Colonial and semi-colonial countries in their fight for national independence and people's democracy.

China agrees with Russia that no African country is truly socialist; they are all waiting to be liberated, and the Chinese view is that this must be brought about by revolu-tion.

Chou En-lai gave expression to the Chinese philosophy when he said at the end of his Africa tour in December 1963 that 'an excellent revolutionary situation existed in Africa'. This could carry a twofold implication: it could imply that the time was ripe for revolutionary wars against the colonial powers in the African territories which are not yet independent. The Russian interpretation of its own policy of peaceful co-existence does not rule this out. But Chou En-lai's statement could also mean that the time was ripe for carrying out 'second degree' revolutions. This in Chinese jargon means getting out the traditional authorities and new élites who now rule Africa, and putting power into the hands of the 'masses'. This 'second degree' socialist revolution is inevitable, according to the Chinese. It should be noted that China has supported militant, anti-imperialist movements in Algeria, Cameroon, Morocco, Guinea, and the Congo. It has also been reported that the Chinese have trained soldiers in Zanzibar, on the Mozambique border, outside Brazzaville, and in the guerrilla academies in Peking to carry out subversion and revolution in Africa. Since Chou En-lai's speech, warnings against subversive activities by China have been given by Niger, Zambia, and Kenya; the revolution in the Congo led by men trained and armed by China has been quelled; Chinese Communists have been turned out of Burundi; and in the Malawi Parliament, Dr. Banda has charged that the Chinese ambassador in Dar-es-Salaam has 'the steering hand' in subversive activities directed against his country. There has been mounting evidence that China is carrying out a campaign of subversion as a matter of policy.

At the same time, she has pursued another policy—a campaign through diplomacy, technical aid, loans, and cultural exchanges to win the friendship and support of African countries for her policies and for the Communist ideology. She has given long-term interest-free loans which she ties to her own imports, and to projects she must approve; consequently, not all the loans are in fact taken up by the governments to which they are offered, but the announcement of the loan has its propaganda value all the same. Economic and technical co-operation agreements, including loans, have been made with Algeria, Ghana, Guinea, Kenya, Mali, Somali, and Tanzania. Chinese official missions of traders, technicians, as well as troupes of acrobats visit one African country or another every year. Chinese experts are teaching Africans to grow rice or other crops in various African countries, such as Guinea, Mali, the Central African Republic, Libya, and Dahomey; and there are Chinese engineers and medical teams in Tanzania and Somali. China's efforts to establish good relations with African countries have also included the exchange of visits and delegations, and the training of African students in China.

But the Soviet Union's economic aid and technical assistance to African countries, her cultural exchanges and facilities for the training of African students have all been on a larger scale than China can afford, and have covered more African countries. Chinese investment in radio and published propaganda has, however, been on a grand scale, and as part of the war between her and the Soviet Union for leadership of the Communist world, and for the control of Africa, she has represented Soviet activities in the fields she cannot rival as part of the policy of 'peaceful co-existence' which the 'white' Soviet Union is carrying out as an ally of the 'imperialists', against the real interests of coloured peoples, at the head of which China places herself.

Despite all this, the pronouncements of the heads of some of the African States have made it clear that they do not consider that Communist ideology fits the social conditions of their countries. In their view, Communist theoreticians do not take sufficient account of the social realities of Africa, even when their own researches disclose them. On

F

the contrary, one expert contradicts the findings of another in their determined efforts to make the facts fit in with Marxist–Leninist doctrine. In illustration, we may refer again to the doctrine of the class struggle. In a study of the Workers' Movement in Africa, Yu N. Popov reached the conclusion that the working class and the national bourgeoisie 'are not at present the chief determinative ones', but that the basic conflicts were 'between the popular masses of Africa and foreign capital'. But Sobilov found the working class 'the most consistent force' in the African liberation movement, and, as we have seen, other experts have found classes in African society, present or emergent, or even to have existed in the past, before the European contacts of the fifteenth century.

As the excerpts from Potekhin have illustrated, some of the Communist theoreticians claim to speak for the 'masses' of Africa when they assert that 'scientific socialism' has been accepted by them as the only way which offers them hope for the future. But this view is not supported by the pronouncements of African leaders who are in a position to speak for their countries.

The Republic of Guinea has received both Soviet and Chinese aid and favour, and is invariably included in their lists of the 'progressive' States of Africa; this means the States which they judge to be moving along the path which leads to 'scientific socialism', in other words, Communism. But President Sekou Touré, though an avowed Marxist, has said that Communism is not the way for Africa, and has rejected some of its basic tenets. He does not agree that the class struggle is necessary, or that religion is reactionary.

The Republic of Mali is another State which both Chinese and Soviet Communists have helped, and regard as 'progressive'. Indeed, President Keita of Mali has publicly expressed his warm gratitude to China, for 'the reasonable cost of her technical assistance and the way in which the technicians adapt themselves to the life of this country'. Nevertheless, Mali, too, has rejected the Communist ideology. At a Conference on 'African ways to Socialism' held in Dakar in December 1962, Dr. Kouyate Seydou, Mali's Minister of Development declared: 'We consider that socialism can be achieved without a Communist Party. We take the view that the political organization of the whole people can bring the country to socialism.' How acceptable to the Communist ideology of China or the Soviet Union is a concept of socialism which excludes both a proletariat and a Communist party? In January 1963 President Keita warned against 'ideological assimilation' by the Communists, and in the following July, the Mali Minister of Education warned against the distribution of propaganda by Chinese diplomats in Mali schools.

Tanzania has accepted aid from China, and the Zanzibar half of it has been under strong Chinese Communist influence; but President Nyerere of Tanzania has warned against a 'second scramble for Africa' between Russia and China for the exploitation of the continent; and Dr. Banda of Malawi has added that the scramble is 'for the soul of Africa' and constituted a grave menace.

Neither the Soviet nor the Chinese version of Communist ideology, confused by their rivalry, charges and counter-charges, and contradictions, nor the new theories or contortions to meet the challenges of African social realities, or placate African critics have won the wide support that the Communists have claimed. During the year 1965 warnings given by the Presidents of the Ivory Coast, Upper Volta,

Niger, Kenya, and Malawi against the dangers of Communism have shown their concern about the threat of Communist subversion to the stability and progress to their States, rather than sanguine hopes for contributions from Communist ideology to democracy.

Soviet and Chinese organizational methods have an appeal in Africa, for all the African countries want rapid industrialization and modernization, and both countries can point to achievements which are impressive. In their search for effective techniques to raise the standards of living of their peoples, some African leaders have turned to the Soviet Union and China, and have sought to copy Communist methods, while rejecting its ideology. But we must ask whether the methods lead to the extension of freedom and democracy, or to its curtailment. One may recall the years between 1929 and 1939 when the Soviet policy of rapid industrialization, and particularly the drive to increase the production of steel, involved the instruments of the secret police to control the population, the building up of a vast bureaucracy, forced labour camps, false trials, and massacres. These are facts which have been admitted by Soviet authorities themselves in their 'De-Stalinization' campaign. But a probing of such methods discloses the nature of Communist democracy. The Chinese drive for rapid industrialization has been accompanied by similar methods and instruments. Communist methods and ideology have little to offer those countries which seek development in freedom.

CHAPTER FIVE

African Concepts of Socialism

African socialism is a compound of several ingredients. It is compounded of reactions to colonialism, capitalism, Marxist–Leninist doctrine, combined with the search for economic development, national sovereignty, democratic freedom and internationalism, and for roots in African tradition and culture. It is therefore not surprising that we should have different admixtures of the various elements to give us different brands of African socialism.

To begin with, the various brands all hark back to the solidarity of traditional African society. In its Sessional Paper on African Socialism, the Kenya Government was at pains to point out that the word 'African' had been introduced to convey 'the African roots of a system that is itself African in its characteristics'.[1] The roots were found in 'two African traditions which form an essential basis for African socialism—political democracy, and mutual social responsibility'. The first 'implies that each member of society is equal in his political rights, and that no individual or group will be permitted to exert undue influence on the policies of the State'; and the second 'implies a mutual responsibility by society and its members to do their very best for each other with the full knowledge and understanding that if society prospers its members will share in that prosperity, and that society cannot prosper without the full co-operation of its members'.

This sense of community and solidarity of traditional African society runs through the various concepts of African socialism. It is the main plank of President Nyerere's concept of socialism as outlined in 'Ujamaa—the basis of African Socialism', an address he gave at Kivukoni College in Dar-es-Salaam in 1962.[2]

He states that African socialism is

rooted in our own past—in the traditional society which produced us. Modern African socialism can draw from its traditional heritage the recognition of 'society' as an extension of the family unit

and he sees socialism essentially as an 'attitude of mind', and

our first step, therefore, is to re-educate ourselves; to regain our former attitude of mind. In our traditional African society we were individuals within a community. We took care of the community, and the community took care of us. We neither needed, nor wished to exploit our fellow men.

The same emphasis on the traditional sense of community appears in President Senghor's concept of African socialism. In his speech at Oxford[3] already referred to, he states:

Thus the working out of our African mode of socialism, the problem is not how to put an end to exploitation of man by his fellow, but to prevent it ever happening, by bringing political and economic democracy back to life; our problem is not how to satisfy spiritual, that is, cultural needs, but how to keep the fervour of the black soul alive.

The solidarity of traditional African society was the fire to be rekindled.

President Modibo Keita of Mali takes up the practical expression of that solidarity. He considers that 'it would be bad policy to break down the traditional pattern of collective life'.[4] He points to the tradition among village communities to join together to work on their farms or on one which they own in common. In the former case, their co-operation makes additional labour available when it is most needed; and in the latter case, they are able to meet community expenses from the produce of the farm they own in common. This traditional practice has been used for constructing roads, schools, bridges, post offices, sports fields, and community centres for which the people have provided voluntary labour. It illustrates the concept of socialism both as a modern approach to economic problems and a continuation of the traditional way of life. One way of looking at African socialism is to see it as a search for effective methods for creating a new social order built on the best traditions of the old, especially on the traditional sense of community and of solidarity between the individual and the group, whereby the welfare of each member was bound up with the welfare of the whole community.

Besides this, there are other objectives which are common elements in the various admixtures of African socialism. They all comprise a reaction to capitalism, especially as experienced under colonial rule, when African labour and produce were exploited for the profit of trading companies of the metropolitan countries of the colonial powers. There is general condemnation of the inequalities and the uneven development associated with the capitalist system. All avow the aim of eliminating or preventing exploitation. For example, President Nyerere's concept of socialism as *Ujamaa* or 'familyhood' is 'opposed to capitalism which seeks to build a happy society on the basis of the exploitation of man by man'.[5] Equally opposed to capitalism is African socialism as espoused by the Kenya Government. Its socialism differs 'from capitalism because it prevents the exercise of disproportionate political influence by economic power groups'.[6]

As was apparent from the statements quoted in the preceding chapter, another common element is the reaction, positive as well as negative, to 'scientific socialism' or Communism. Some African spokesmen describe their brand of socialism as 'African' while others, like Ghana, Guinea, and Mali, disavow the terminology and prefer 'scientific socialism', but they all insist that their brands of socialism are not identical with any European form of scientific socialism. There are basic tenets which they reject.

As was shown in the preceding chapter, the rejection of the doctrine of class struggle is almost unanimous. In the Kenya Government's Sessional Paper, it is specifically stated that the class divisions of Europe have no parallel in African society, and that the class problem of Africa is largely one of prevention; in particular, to eliminate the risk of foreign domination, or the emergence of antagonistic classes.[7]

President Nyerere also denies the existence of classes in traditional African society. He doubts 'if the equivalent of the word "class" exists in any indigenous African language, for language describes the ideas of those who speak it, and the idea of "class" or "caste" was non-existent in African society'.[8]

These views based on East African societies are similar

to those held of West African societies. In his exposition of African socialism, President Senghor describes traditional West African societies as classless, and with no wage-earning sector.[9]

In these concepts of socialism the class struggle associated with socialism elsewhere has no place, but one exception should be noted. Contrary to the view on which most African spokesmen are agreed that African society had no class stratification, the Ghana paper, *The Spark*,[10] espoused in 1963 ideas which followed orthodox Communist doctrine. It asserted that 'classes do exist in Africa both in the sense of economic groups occupying different portions in the productive system (that is as employers, self-employed workers, etc.) and in the sense of different income groups'. It was made clear why the paper took this line. The reason was ideological, for the paper itself disclosed 'the denial of the existence of these classes is ultimately a denial of the need for socialism in Africa'. In conformity with orthodox doctrine, *The Spark* could not conceive socialism without a class struggle. If in this it propounded the policy of the Government of Ghana, then the policy had changed by 1964, for *Consciencism*[11] published that year, shows that Nkrumah's Marxist socialism accepted the communalism of traditional African society to be the foundation of his brand of socialism; he denied the existence of classes, and rejected the class struggle, and the inevitability of revolution. But there was a shift of emphasis on Pan-Africanism as an indispensable ingredient of his socialism. He has the Trotsky conception that socialism cannot succeed unless it embraces the whole continent of Africa. That the political kingdom comes first is reflected in this conception, the instrument of which, as advocated, should be a single continental party as the vanguard of socialism. No other African country supports this concept of socialism.

Attention may be drawn to African reaction to another fundamental Marxist tenet of socialism: the State ownership of the means of production, distribution, and exchange. African socialism is not wholly committed to this doctrine. It is the stated aim of Ghana (under Nkrumah), Guinea, and Mali to build Marxist Socialist States, but in all African countries, including these three, the approach to nationalization is pragmatic, dictated by the situation in which they must carry out their programmes of economic development. The approach of the Kenya Government exemplifies the general attitude. It has declared that it is not committed to indiscriminate nationalization, but will be guided by such considerations as cost, profitability, or necessity. It will resort to nationalization

only where the national security is threatened, high social benefits can be obtained, or productive resources are seriously and clearly being misused, where other means of control are ineffective, and financial resources permit, or where a service is vital to the Government as part of its responsibility to the nation.[12]

But all have State enterprises, though some have more than others. Ghana, Guinea, and Mali have established more State enterprises in their respective States, bringing more sectors of their economies under public ownership or control than other States in West Africa have done; but compared with countries in the region which have similar resources, such as Nigeria, Ivory Coast, or Mauretania, the States with more State enterprises fare worse in terms of losses and rates of economic growth. Ghana, which is richer than Guinea or Mali, has been showing considerable losses from State enterprises. In the 1963-4 Financial Year, there were thirty-five State-owned companies operating in Ghana. Three of them could not present accounts of their operations; the remaining thirty-two showed between them losses which amounted to £14 million. The total investment in all the companies was £40 million; so in a single year over one-third of the invested capital was lost. The Ghana Finance Minister attributed the heavy losses to 'high wage and salary bills, inexperienced management, lack of proper accounting and control within the enterprises, under utilization of plant capacity, and inadequate sales promotion'. Guinea which also embarked on extensive nationalization had to change its policy after two years because the enterprises did not add to national wealth, but on the contrary increased the economic difficulties. Such experiences justify the pragmatic approach to State ownership. The Kenya Government policy that nationalization will be considered 'if the need is urgent, if other less costly controls are ineffective, and if it is understood that most industries will not be operated at a loss,'[13] is the more representative of the approach of African governments to State ownership.

The achievement of rapid economic development to increase national wealth, to raise standards of living, and to enable governments to provide much needed services such as education, hospitals, employment, old age or unemployment benefits, and the social security associated with the modern Welfare State are objectives avowed by all the African States. We may again quote from the statement of the Kenya Government:

The ultimate objectives of all societies are remarkably similar and have a universal character suggesting that present conflicts need not be enduring. These objectives typically include: (i) political equality; (ii) social justice; (iii) human dignity including freedom of conscience; (iv) freedom from want, disease and exploitations; (v) equal opportunities; and (vi) high and growing *per capita* incomes, equitably distributed. Different societies attach different weights and priorities to these objectives, but it is largely in the political and economic means adopted for achieving these ends that societies differ. These differences in means are, however, of paramount importance because ultimate objectives are never fully attained. Every time one target is attained a new one becomes necessary. Indeed, we forever live in transition.[14]

The statement sketches the broad setting within which, through varying orders of priority and admixtures, the particular characteristics of African brands of socialism are evolving.

The problems posed by the common desire for rapid economic development have caused all the African States to accept economic planning as the only practicable policy. This assigns to governments the undisputed responsibility to provide leadership by directing and instituting appropriate measures and controls for the development and use of a nation's human and natural resources for the benefit of the whole society, by the most modern scientific methods. Certain common features are discernible in the efforts being made by respective African governments to discharge the obligations imposed by this undisputed responsibility.

All the African States need capital and skills from outside. They have therefore adopted policies which allow room for private enterprises which bring them the skills, machinery, and foreign exchange which they need. This has led to the evolution of a pattern in which private capital, increasingly in the form of joint enterprises with the State, is playing an important role in the economic development of Africa. Most African countries have entered into trade and economic agreements with countries both of the East and West. Whether they avow socialism or not, African countries have established mixed economies based on State and private ownership. Paradoxically, it is Western capitalism that is being employed to finance African socialism. This is most evident in the countries which have announced that they are building Marxist Socialist States. Ghana provides a good illustration of the paradox. A recent report by the World Bank has given a table of investments in Ghana from 1959 to 1964. The figures were[15]:

The West

Great Britain	£80 million	
West Germany	£40 million	
United States	£30 million	
France	£10 million	TOTAL: £160 million

The East

Soviet Union	£15 million	
Poland	£10 million	
People's Republic of China	£2 million	TOTAL: £27 million

Thus over 85 per cent of the investments over the last five years came from Western capital; the development of Marxism–Leninism in Ghana is heavily dependent on the capitalist systems of the West.

Both Russia and China decry the economic links between Africa and the West; Russia would like to replace them with links between herself and Africa; but China would disrupt the links, even if she cannot herself fill the vacuum.

Both countries teach that socialism cannot be genuine as long as this heavy reliance on the capitalist countries of the West remains. The African States, however, in accordance with their declared policies of non-alignment are collaborating with Western capital, and this has to be accepted as a common feature of African socialism.

Other common features are noticeable. All the African countries are building, according to their respective resources, the infra-structure of roads, communications, electric power, and other public services necessary for economic growth. Also, they all emphasize the development of agriculture not only to provide more food or increase the export crops on which their foreign exchanges mainly depend but also because agriculture is an important component of the infra-structure necessary to sustain industrial development. The Kenya Government holds up its plans for agriculture as the best example of African socialism at work, since 'every form of organization will be utilized, including national farms, co-operatives, companies, partnerships, and individual farms'.[16]

The emphasis on education is another common feature. All kinds of educational facilities from primary school to university are being rapidly extended. African States regard education as a profitable investment, the key to the problem of manpower. Economic growth as well as public and welfare services depend on skilled and trained personnel which is in inadequate supply throughout Africa.

It can also be said that African socialism shares a common internationalism. It is fair to see this as in part related to African poverty and need. Africa cannot develop in isolation; the modernization on which the various States have embarked requires financial and technical assistance, and moreover, modern methods of production and distribution impel international co-operation. This fact is accepted by all African States; what they wish to avoid is domination by foreign countries through political and/or economic ties.

The internationalism has been related to traditional structures and attitudes, as, for example, by President Nyerere when he states:

> The tradition and the objective of African socialism is the extended family. The true African socialist does not look on one class of man as his brethren and another as his natural enemies. He does not form an alliance with the 'brethren' for the extermination of the 'non-brethren'. He rather regards all men as his brethren—as members of his ever-extending family.[17]

Viewed against the background of African history, this is idealism; but it is an idealism which gives support to the compulsions of practical realities.

The co-ordination of the felt needs and desires in practicable programmes requires scientific research to collect basic statistics about a particular society and its resources, to assess potentialities for new industries, and to make forecasts for forward planning. Planning and scientific research are features of the policies of African countries, whether they call themselves socialist or not. To these may be added techniques to diffuse ownership, through State enterprises, co-operatives, joint ventures in which State and private capital co-operate, and the various measures of control through various forms of taxation. These are all elements which in varying degrees are embodied in the programmes and policies of African countries.

Socialist ingredients vary from one African country to another. They all claim to be aiming at the equitable distribution of wealth, and at social justice and freedom. There are in every country traces of trends and ideas usually associated with socialism: the development of co-operatives, the desire to avoid inequalities and exploitation, the sense of community which seeks expression in mutual responsibility and collective welfare, the stress on social justice, political equality, and international co-operation. These values are not the exclusive monopoly of socialism, but any country which professes them can claim to be socialist. Professions and aspirations must be measured against practice. It is the point at which socialism must be tested.

In specific relation to democracy, African countries include freedom and social justice among their objectives. The literature on African socialism contains criticisms of Communism because its methods destroy equality and freedom in the name of the 'dictatorship of the proletariat'. President Senghor is a prominent exponent of this view. He contends that

in communist countries, 'the dictatorship of the proletariat', contrary to the teachings of Marx has made the State an omnipotent, soulless monster, stifling the natural freedoms of the human being, and drying up the sources of art, without which life is not worth living.[18]

Profession and practice, however, often diverge as we show in the chapter on democracy. We may note here in connection with socialism that a centrally planned economy can be an instrument of oppression. It expands the power of the new ruling élite, and they can use it to destroy both social justice and freedom which are professed as central features of socialism. We have examples of this in the re-

strictions on trade-union freedom in many African countries, notably in Ghana and Guinea which avow Marxism.

There are in many States a growing gap between the new
rulers, politicians, civil servants, and military personnel and
the mass of the population both in urban and rural areas.
This is most conspicuous in the poor States with economies
that are scarcely viable. Poverty and the growing gap between privileged party bosses, politicians, and government
employees on the one hand, and the bulk of the population
on the other, underlie the discontent which has culminated
in the military coups of Dahomey, the Central African Republic, and Upper Volta, December 1965–January 1966. But
the phenomenon is not confined to these countries. Trade-
union leaders in other African countries, including the
Congo Republics, Ghana, and Nigeria have warned against
the growing inequalities between the privileged members of
the new régimes and the industrial and agricultural
workers in towns and villages. There is evidence of uneven
distribution that does not conform to the claims of socialism.

It may also be pointed out that while the values of solidarity and mutual responsibility of traditional small-scale
societies are extolled as the basis of the modern socialist
philosophies of Africa, the institutions in which these
values were given expression, such as the lineage or tribe
are decried, or are being irresistibly destroyed by development programmes and by the processes of social change.
There is a problem of giving new institutional expression to
the cherished values.

Finally, we may note the moral and religious aspects of
African socialism. Socialism in Europe has been inspired
not only by economic goals but even more by spiritual and

G

moral ones—by the goals of social justice, equality, fraternity, and humanity which gave it momentum. Where these dry up, socialism loses its substance. African socialism also derives its inspiration from moral and spiritual values. We have already noted the policy of the Kenya Government that religion will be a prominent feature of its African socialism because it was a force which provided 'a strict moral code for the community'. The same government has stated that the goals of political equality, social justice, and human dignity will not be sacrificed to achieve material ends more quickly, and that socialism includes a 'merciless fight against social dishonesties and injustices, against excessive wages, and the fraudulent conversion of public funds'. It also lays emphasis on the need for discipline—'if discipline is rejected, so is planning, and with it, African socialism'.

Another example of the ethical basis of African socialism is given by President Nyerere's statement that wealth and the power it gives should not be used to dominate and exploit others. This is regarded as incompatible with socialism.[19] What true African socialism must preserve and apply within the wider society of the nation is 'the socialist attitude of mind which in the tribal days, gave to every individual the security that comes from belonging to a widely extended family'. Similarly, Mr. Mamadou Dias, when as President of the Council of Ministers he addressed the National Assembly of the Republic of Senegal on the anniversary of Independence Day on April 4th, 1961, spoke of a genuine African socialism 'which leads us towards the realization of this socialist society by infusing into it our African values'. These are the values of the common good and healthy forms of community life.

We aim at developing a new type of man, inspired by an awareness of the world and also by a sense of the spiritual values of the forces of life whose rhythm forms our aesthetic valuation.... This spiritual humanism will be in harmony with the Christian as well as the Moslem way of life, for we are in a profound sense a people of believers.... Our African socialism is not a scholastic theory but a vital challenge and hence also an ethic and an obligation.[20]

The concepts of African socialism, as the foregoing has shown, are complex compounds. They represent a search for rational methods of social development and social order, and for the expression of national sovereignty and the dignity of the African; they reflect reactions to colonialism, and to European ideologies; they express faith in spiritual values and in the brotherhood of all mankind. The various compounds admixed by the different States are not uniform in content, for the search is still at its beginnings; nor do they describe accomplished social facts, for they include ideals and aspirations, judged by which the contemporary situations show many failings, and even contradictions. They avow certain values which they share in common with European concepts of socialism, but they are not identical with them, for the search is for distinctive expressions in the context of the history and social conditions of Africa.

As far as democracy is concerned, socialism, of whatever admixture, has dangers to which attention must be drawn. Socialism is beneficial when it is democratic; but it can exist without democracy, and then it can be very despotic. The State ownership and control of economic enterprises leads to the concentration of both political and economic power in the hands of those who are governing, from the big bosses at the top, through the whole range of officialdom to the smallest organization. Experience has shown that men who come to have such power can use it to enrich themselves, to deny employment to others, to arrest and imprison them, and to impose all kinds of restrictions and punishments in order to have their own way. They can crush their opponents, and all who do not do as they command. Power under socialism needs to be decentralized and widely distributed; there should be effective checks on those who rule; individual citizens must have safeguards, institutions, and laws which protect them against tyranny; without such checks, socialism can be an instrument of appalling despotism and dictatorship. What we learn of the 'New Imperialism' in the Soviet Union and China, and other socialist countries behind the Iron Curtain warns us of the terrible dangers of socialism without democracy.[21] Some African countries, such as Ghana, are already on the road where the wrecks of freedom and justice are warning signposts. Socialism in essence is a moral doctrine which rests on human dignity and social justice. Its perversion becomes frightening oppression and tyranny.

CHAPTER SIX

The Ingredients of Democracy

In the second chapter where we discussed the political heritage of Africa before the period of European colonization,
we endeavoured to show that some tribal political systems
possessed essential elements of democracy, with checks and
balances to prevent arbitrary authoritarianism; and in the
third chapter we closed our brief survey of the impact of
colonialism with the remark that the colonial powers left a
legacy of ideas and techniques which could help any
country whose leaders wished to establish democratic forms
of government. Western democratic ideas are threads in the
texture of democracy being woven in Africa.

The difficulty about democracy is that countries with
quite different political ideologies use the same word to describe their respective systems. This is no less true of Africa
than of Europe where countries both of the 'East' and
'West' claim to be democratic. President Sekou Touré of
Guinea is reported to have said:

There are two ways of governing a country. In the first way,
the State may substitute itself for all initiative, all men, all con-
sciences. At that moment it deprives the people of their liberty
of initiative, places them under conditions, and in consequence
passes itself as omniscient by trying to solve general problems

and problems of detail simultaneously. Such a State can only be anti-democratic and oppressive. We have adopted the second way and chosen to be a democratic State.[1]

Guinea is a Marxist-inspired one-party State which does not allow the legal existence of an organized opposition. The institutions of democracy are not the same everywhere. We have to examine the values.

On the other hand, President Azikiwe has also written of Nigeria:

> The domestic policy of Nigeria will be framed on the assumption that Nigeria shall continue to be a Parliamentary democracy. The Government of Nigeria shall exercise power so long as it retains the confidence of the legislature. It will express its belief in parliamentary democracy as government by discussion, based on the consent of the governed, whose will is collectively expressed by the duly accredited representatives of an electorate that is based on a universal adult suffrage and that votes by secret ballots at periodic elections.[2]

By contrast with what obtains in Guinea, President Azikiwe goes on to say that democracy must include a recognized opposition, and that without the opposition, 'democracy becomes a sham'. He also insists on two other ingredients as essential for democracy: the Rule of Law, and the enforcement of fundamental Human Rights.

We may best approach the concepts of democracy in Africa by looking for the ingredients which African leaders have accepted as contents of the term. It should be borne in mind that democracy expresses both principles and ideals; principles which those who believe in democracy wish to be given practical expression in the laws and institutions of society; and ideals which provide goals towards which men in society should constantly aspire for the betterment of society.

Democracy is founded on respect for the human being—every human being. This is one of the ideas of democracy which all the African States accept. It implies the acceptance of racial equality. On it is based the claim that all who have been victims of racial prejudice should be admitted to full citizenship in their societies to enjoy, without discrimination, the full rights of democratic citizenship. The wide agreement on this principle is shown by the unanimous condemnation by African States of minority governments in South Africa, Rhodesia, and the Portuguese colonies of Angola and Mozambique, in all of which there are threatening tensions between those who enjoy the full rights of democratic citizenship, and those to whom these rights have been denied. The principle was expressed most authoritatively at an African Conference on the Rule of Law which was organized by the International Commission of Jurists in Lagos, Nigeria, from January 3rd to 7th, 1961. The 194 participants were all jurists, judges, teachers of law, and practising lawyers from twenty-three African countries, and nine other countries of Asia, Europe, and North America. The conference afforded an opportunity for a free and frank discussion and exchange of views, and among the principles on which all the participants agreed were that 'the Rule of Law cannot be fully realized unless legislative bodies have been established in accordance with the will of the people who have adopted their Constitution freely', and that 'Governments should adhere to the system of democratic representation in their legislatures'. The case against the governments of South Africa, Rhodesia, and the Portuguese colonies of Angola and Mozambique is that they do not conform to these principles, and that by implication they deny the racial equality and the dignity of the human being on which democracy rests. The Unilateral Declaration of Independence by which the white government of Rhodesia which represents only one-fourteenth of the population has seized independence in order to rule over the larger African population is similarly a flagrant violation of this fundamental principle of democracy.

Respect for the dignity of man carries other implications besides the principle that the dignity of all men should be equally respected. Democracy has other values which derive from the same source. Every man, according to democratic belief, should have certain civil liberties without which no social order can be characterized as democratic. Within broad limits, every man should have a say in how he is governed, and by whom he is governed; he should be free to criticize his government, and be protected from arbitrary action against him by his government; he should be free to express his views, according to his own lights; he should be free to associate with others with whom he chooses to associate, in order to gain a better hearing for his views, or register his complaints, or seek to improve his conditions; a citizen needs this right especially when he is in a minority, be it racial, political, or social; every man should be free to travel and to move about as he wishes, or to practise his own religion, or to bring up his children according to his beliefs. A citizen in a democratic system must at least be assured of his freedom of speech, of assembly, of conscience and of the person. These are liberties befitting the dignity of man in democratic society. They have been best expressed in the U.N. Declaration of Human Rights to which, as appears below, references are frequently made.

We have seen how in some traditional political systems there were institutions for the choice and deposition of rulers, and for the expression of grievances, and for their settlement. These were not enshrined in constitutions but were based on tradition. In the contemporary situation, the new States of Africa have sought to guarantee civil liberties and fundamental human rights in Constitutions. Some examples of these may be cited:

The Independence Constitution of Nigeria (1960) made among other things the following provisions for civil liberties—

(1) the right to life—against anyone being arbitrarily deprived of life;

(2) freedom from inhuman treatment; so as to ensure, for example, that no Nigerian citizen is in any way subjected to any form of bodily or mental torture, whether to extract confessions from an accused person, or from a witness in a judicial proceeding, or in any other circumstances of domestic life;

(3) freedom from slavery or forced labour;

(4) the right to liberty and security of person;

(5) rights concerning civil and criminal law, providing for fair and impartial administration of justice in an open court, and enjoining that everyone charged with a criminal offence should be presumed innocent until proved guilty according to law;

(6) the right to private and family life (as in article 8 of the Convention on Human Rights);

(7) rights concerning religion (as in article 9 of the

Convention on Human Rights) guaranteeing freedom of thought, conscience, and religion, including freedom to choose one's religion or belief, and the right to propagate it;

(8) right to freedom of expression—that everyone is free to say or write what he likes so long as the same is not defamatory, seditious, obscene, or blasphemous;

(9) freedom of peaceful association and assembly, including the right 'to form and join trade or other unions for the protection of one's interests';

(10) freedom of movement and residence; under which it is provided that no citizen of Nigeria can be deported from Nigeria;

(11) right to compensation for the compulsory acquisition of property;

(12) the enjoyment of fundamental rights without discrimination; and

(13) freedom from discriminatory legislation.[8]

These are the same liberties which any democratic country of the West would secure for her citizens. Even when the Constitution breaks down, as it has done in Nigeria (1966), the ideals remain as a challenge to fresh efforts.

The Constitutions of the new States of Uganda and Kenya contain in each case a Bill of Rights which guarantees equality before the law, personal freedom, freedom of belief and conscience, freedom of movement, the free choice of domicile, and the right to property; and prohibits slavery and forced labour, torture, and cruel or inhuman or degrading treatment and punishment. To these, Kenya adds the 'right to leave Kenya' thus recognizing the right of persons to leave any country, including their own, to be one of the basic freedoms.[4] Again, these conform to the democratic values of the West.

We may note that some of the French-speaking States of Africa make similar provisions for civil liberties in their Constitutions. The Constitution of the Republic of Senegal specifies in Articles 6 to 20, rights and freedoms similar to those enumerated above, and adds the right to work, to education, and to the protection of the family. Another instance is the Constitution of the Republic of Mali which affirms in the preamble the rights and liberties of man and of the citizen 'consecrated by the Universal Declaration of Human Rights of December 10th, 1948'.

Democracy cannot work unless those who seek to exercise these civil liberties recognize the equal rights of others to exercise them too. They must recognize the right of others to think differently, and to choose differently. In traditional societies, all members held the same religious beliefs, shared in the same rituals, held the same views about the universe. The highly valued solidarity of traditional society was based on conformity; but it is old-fashioned to hope to achieve solidarity on the basis of conformity in the circumstances of today. In the contemporary situation, a State consists of people holding different religious views— Catholics, Protestants, Moslems, or animists; they may hold different views not only in religion but also in science or philosophy, or politics, and in other ideologies or subjects. It is assumed that they can all nevertheless agree on the validity of the ideals of democracy and be equally loyal to them. Where there are opportunities of wide contacts and of access to different ideas, there are occasions for different opinions and beliefs. Therefore, an important requirement for the success of democracy is *tolerance*, and it can be said to be one of the most important characteristics of democratic society. The late President Olympio of Togo showed penetrating incisiveness when he said that

the test of a democratic régime in Africa might not necessarily be the actual presence of a second party or several parties, so much as whether or not the régime tolerated individualists. This is the crucial point, for societies are not built or improved by conformists.[5]

There are other compelling reasons for tolerance in a democracy. Democratic societies accept the view that all human beings are fallible. No one is omniscient; no one has a monopoly of truth; no one embodies or expresses the will of the whole people. Those who govern may command wide popularity at a particular period, but that will not prevent them from erring, through misunderstanding, or lack of sufficient knowledge, or self-delusion, or corruption, or insensitiveness, so that they do not care how their actions affect others. In Lord Acton's famous and oft-quoted sentence: 'Power tends to corrupt, and absolute power tends to corrupt absolutely.' Consequently, a democratic society provides methods and institutions for the preservation of liberty. These include such organs as newspapers, trade unions and other voluntary associations, political parties, and an elected parliament which has continual opportunity for criticizing those who rule, and for expressing the views of the governed. All these require tolerance for their proper functioning.

Democracy is government by consent. Public discussion, free elections, the right of freedom of speech and association are regarded as essential because they are necessary for achieving consent. It is in this context that the citizen's right to vote in free elections has rightly been singled out in Africa for emphasis, particularly in those societies where whites who are in the minority rule over the majority. The cry is 'one man, one vote'. But it should be noted that this is valueless without freedom of speech and association or public discussion.

The right to vote is important because democracy is a system of choosing. The words of the famous speech which President Lincoln of America delivered at Gettysburg on November 19th, 1863: 'that this nation, under God, shall have a new birth of freedom—and that government of the people, by the people, for the people, shall not perish from the earth' have echoed throughout Africa, and have been interpreted as epitomizing not only the political creed of American democracy but of all democratic States. Modern States, including those in Africa, are too large for every member to participate in making decisions on the functions of government; the small, primary lineage no longer encompasses the whole of the political community; but all can take part in electing by majority vote those who are given authority to govern as representatives of all the people. If the vote is to be meaningful, it must offer a choice; it must be a selection from competing individuals or groups.

Democracy caters for pluralistic societies. This is noteworthy because the States of present-day Africa are composed of pluralistic societies. They consist not only of different religious groups but also of many different ethnic groups, and a growing number of different associations, such as trade unions, farmers', traders', youth, or women's associations, and the like. The individuals who join these associations do so because they promote or protect some particular interest or interests of theirs. In modern societies most individuals need the protection and support of one social group or another, and there are many who join more than one group, because no single group caters for all their various interests. This is a boon which democratic societies welcome and encourage because it means that no one is totally dependent on any single organization. Such total dependence threatens freedom and democracy, for it would mean the exercise of monopolistic power over the individual. For example, the State should not be the only employer, for this would give it too much power over the lives of the citizens; State power should be checked by the existence of other employers. Similarly, the individual should be protected against the private employer by his Union or the State. A democratic society which is based on government by consent should make it possible for individuals to join any groups they like, and for the groups to be able to promote the interests they represent. But no group should be above criticism and no group, political or economic, should be monolithic.

Sociologists who have concerned themselves with social processes have pointed out that competition and conflict are as inherent in human association as are accommodation and co-operation. One of the characteristics of democratic societies of the West is that they have institutional arrangements which give recognition to the fact that disagreement and conflict of interests are present in society. The major institutional arrangement is provided by the party system which brings conflict out into the open and provides a legal and social framework for dealing with it. The existence of political parties as an instrument of political rivalry not only allows for the expression of dissent but also offers the people a choice of alternatives.

It should be noted that in the context of the countries of the West which have accepted and maintained the party system, the legal opposition is not a source of social instability or disunity; on the contrary, it promotes social cohesion. It does this because it enables dissent to be legitimately and constructively expressed, subjects those in power to constant criticism, protects minority interests, and makes sure that the rulers understand and try to realize the general interest of all, as far as is possible. Those in opposition are given opportunity through service on committees, through consultation and through debate to contribute to the general interest. Thus the opposition helps to make all citizens, including those who disagree with the party in power, a part of the democratic system. The party system and the opposition are a part of the machinery of government. This aspect is brought out, because there are those in Africa who represent the opposition as a vehicle of disunity. The argument is fallacious. The toleration of opposition is regarded by the West as a high democratic virtue. Its existence means there is a choice; and the point of an election is to give citizens the opportunity to exercise that choice.

The institution of different political parties, and the recognition of an opposition are aspects of Western democracy which many African States do not accept to be essential for democracy. In some of them the opposition has been forcibly liquidated, or abolished by law; in others, it has been cajoled or intimidated into joining the party in power; and in still others it is permitted by law, but weakly survives, because of the strength and popularity of the party in power. For different reasons, it seems that the opposition as an organized, legal, and tolerated party is on the decline in Africa. As we have seen, President Azikiwe regarded a recognized opposition as an essential part of the democratic system; but the *coup* in Nigeria (January 1966) has brought a military government into power; the Constitution has now been temporarily suspended, and along with it the democratic institutions of parties and parliament. One may also refer to the 1962 Constitution of Morocco which stated that political parties contributed to the representation of citizens in the government, and provided against one-party rule in the third article that 'there shall be no single party in Morocco'.[6] In the same year, U Thant, then Acting Secretary-General of the United Nations, made a speech which offered the following view:

The notion that democracy requires the existence of an organized opposition to the government of the day is not valid. Democracy requires only freedom for opposition, not necessarily its organized existence. In many newly independent countries it is most unlikely that there will be a two-party system for many years to come. The nationalist movements are powerful indeed. They will control governments without there being any effective challenge to them from within. And any challenge from outside would merely strengthen them. As was the case in many European countries, it might take some time before it would be possible for political opposition to be expressed in constitutional forms.[7]

This explanation concedes freedom for an opposition. The notable fact is that some African States have taken steps to establish one-party States which deny that freedom. But not all African States accept that development: Gabriel d'Arboussier, the Minister of Justice of the Republic of Senegal, writing on the significance of the Lagos Conference of 1961 stated:

Fully aware that sectarianism and imposed intellectual and moral guidance are often factors of stagnation and obscurantism, Africa intends to benefit by progress derived from freedom of thought and expression combined with intellectual daring and integrity. Political opposition must, therefore, be legally recognized as long as it does not seek to impose its will through methods of brute force which are in themselves a negation of freedom.[8]

The place of an organized opposition as part of the democratic system is still a controversial issue in Africa. We return to it in the chapter on one-party States.

By common agreement, one of the essentials of democracy is the Rule of Law. The International Commission of Jurists has defined this as

adherence to those institutions and procedures, not always identical, but broadly similar, which experience and tradition in the different countries of the world, often having themselves varying political structures and economic backgrounds, have shown to be essential to protect the individual from arbitrary government and to enable him to enjoy the dignity of man.[9]

An authoritative African view of the Rule of Law was put by the Chief Justice of Nigeria, Sir Adeokunbo A. Ademola, at the Lagos Conference. He said:

The Rule of Law is not a Western idea, nor is it linked up with any economic or social system. As soon as you accept that man is governed by Law and not by the whims of man, it is the Rule of Law. It may be under different forms from country to country, but it is based on principles; it is not an abstract notion. It exists not only in democratic countries, but in every country where the law is supreme, where the dignity of man is respected and provision made for his legitimate rights. Today, around us we see countries where basic principles are disregarded, where

H

there are cases of arbitrary arrests and detentions without trial; cases of the repression of the Opposition in parliamentary government; cases of negation of social and political rights; cases of the Judiciary stifled and paralysed by fear and dismissal of the judges. When we look around we find some of these encroachments of the Executive on the rights of individuals ... in countries ostensibly practising democracy, but in actual fact the individual is subject to such restrictions which deprive him almost completely of his freedom.[10]

It is one thing to accept the Rule of Law as a democratic principle; it is another thing to provide institutions for implementing it. In a democracy, the Rule of Law places limitations on the power of the government in the interest of personal freedom. One of the things on which all the jurists at the Lagos Conference agreed was that there was need for an independent Judiciary, if the Rule of Law was to be a reality. In the Soviet Union, for example, the Constitution enunciates principles of the Rule of Law; but there are no effective guarantees in the judicial machinery for its democratic exercise. The Judiciary is not independent; in practice, it is subject to the supreme will of the ruling party.[11]

Many African countries have accepted the principle of the independence of the Judiciary. The majority of the French-speaking States have adopted in their Constitutions, the same 'notion of judicial authority' as the French Constitution of October 4th, 1948; Senegal, Mauretania, Upper Volta, Dahomey, Ivory Coast, the Congo, Niger, Gabon, and Chad have all affirmed the principle of the independence of the Judiciary, as have Guinea, Togo, the Cameroons and Morocco. In all of them, 'the Judiciary is an authority independent of the Executive and the Legislature'. The same is true of Nigeria, Sierra Leone, Kenya, and Uganda. We may recall a speech delivered by Mr. Isaac Forster, President of the Supreme Court of Senegal at its inaugural session on November 14th, 1960. Present at the ceremony were the Presidents of the Malagasy Republic, and of the Republic of Senegal, other dignitaries of the Republic, and representatives of the diplomatic corps. Mr. Forster said:

We Senegalese can bear calmly and without embarrassment the spotlight turned on us, for it lights up only institutions which are absolutely democratic. Indeed, the governments which you represent should be reassured by the example I am giving you at this very moment of the independence of Senegal's Judiciary. Have you often seen, anywhere else, a judge take the liberties which I am taking now, in the presence of the President of the Republic, the Prime Minister, the President of the National Assembly, not to mention my own Minister, the Minister of Justice? Have you often heard anywhere else, a judge declare publicly to the Executive: 'If your statutory deeds are illegal, we shall rescind them', and to the Legislature, 'If your laws are unconstitutional, we shall oppose their promulgation'? What better guarantees could we offer to even the most sceptical amongst you? [12]

The Independence of the Judiciary is, however, in jeopardy in at least two African States, Mali and Ghana. In Mali, a 'People's Court' was set up in July 1962 to try agitators arrested in connection with demonstrations against measures of monetary reform introduced by the government. The People's Court of thirty-nine members consisted of a presiding judge, a delegate from each of the thirty local sections of the one party, the Union Soudanaise, and two delegates from each of the women's, young people's, trade unions, and veterans' organizations. The judicial provisions of the Republic of Mali had not included such a People's Court, but it is significant that early in December 1962, speaking at the closing session of a seminar of Mali judges, the President said:

Judges of the Republic of Mali must not be led, in the name of the independence of the Judiciary and the separation of powers, to lose sight of the fact that they are first and foremost militant members of the Union Soudanaise.... For all militant members of the Union Soudanaise, the Judiciary, as a social institution of the State and a supreme body by its very nature, must necessarily be in the service of the régime which established it.[13]

In Ghana, a Special Court set up by law in 1961 consisted of a presiding judge and two other members sitting without a jury. Its jurisdiction extended to offences against the safety of the State, offences against the peace, and offences specified by the President. The Court was constituted by the Chief Justice in accordance with a request made to him by the President. In 1963 the Special Court tried five persons on allegations of treason. Two of them were former Ministers of the Nkrumah government, and one was the Executive Secretary of his party, the Convention People's Party. The Court acquitted the three members of the Convention People's Party. The President thereupon dismissed the Chief Justice, and got the legislature to vote him powers to set aside the verdicts of the Special Court. The legislature duly obeyed, and the President set aside the verdicts. A new law was passed which enabled the President to dismiss judges of the High Court and the Supreme Court in the same way as he dismissed the Chief Justice. In October 1964 the five defendants were tried again on the same charges before the special Criminal Division of the High Court, presided over by the new Chief Justice. None of them was represented by Counsel. All of them were found guilty and sentenced to death on February 9th, 1965. Six weeks later, the President announced that he had commuted the sentences to twenty years' imprisonment. A statement comparable to the one made by the President of Mali just quoted above was propounded by Radio Ghana to the effect that 'The Judiciary is an organ of society and in our society the people are supreme; hence the institutions of our society can enjoy autonomy only up to the point that they serve the highest ideals of society'.[14] Offences against the State were made triable by a Special Court consisting of judges whom the President could dismiss at his discretion, and the judgement of the Court could also be set aside at the President's discretion. This was a complete rejection of the independence of the Judiciary which most other African States have accepted as an essential element of democracy.

A final point which may be made about democracy is that it ultimately rests on the morality and discipline of the citizens. A democracy in the last analysis depends on the character of individual men and women and the moral standards of the community. Rules governing elections may be made; freedoms may be provided in constitutions; and Bills of Right may be passed; they will make arbitrary acts easier to resist publicly, but they will not by themselves secure democracy. There are other rules which are unwritten, such as honesty, integrity, restraint, and respect for democratic procedures. We could add an impartial and incorrupt civil service, or the willingness to serve in voluntary organizations, all of which call for moral standards and good behaviour.

This aspect of democracy is realized and accepted by

African leaders. Here are two examples. During a debate in the National Assembly at Dar-es-Salaam, fears were expressed regarding the strong executive powers which were provided for the President in the new Constitution. President Nyerere was reported to have replied that the ultimate safeguards of the people's rights and freedom were not the Constitution, but the 'ethic of the nation'. It was impossible to devise a Constitution which would be foolproof against a tyrant. 'We must put faith in some human being. I know members have questioned the idea of faith, but democracy is a declaration of faith in human nature.'[15]

The second example is from an article written by Tom Mboya, now Minister of Economic Development of Kenya. He wrote: 'Africa's struggle has been based on moral issues and in defence of basic democratic human rights and fundamental freedoms. ... Africa ought to remain the symbol and reminder to the world of dedication to freedom and democracy.'[16]

It has often been stated both by Africans and Europeans that Africa should not be expected to have a 'Westminster type democracy'. One interpretation given to this seems to imply that Africans are incapable of practising democratic rule. If this refers to the values of democracy, such as the rule of law, respect for human dignity, or the freedoms of speech, association, conscience, and the other ingredients of democracy we have referred to in this chapter, it can be seen from the evidence that Africans cherish democratic values, and that there are leaders whose political policies are inspired by them. The values of democracy must be seen as ideals which have universal validity.

Another interpretation of the statement is that Africans cannot be expected to adopt the same institutions as those of Westminster. This is, in fact, not saying something that is new; it has historical and sociological support. Countries borrow ideas and institutions from one another. Africa has already borrowed many ideas and institutions from Europe, including political institutions like the party, and political offices like Prime Minister, Minister, or President, and other institutions like schools and trade unions. The sociological fact is that institutions borrowed from one country into another are never exactly the same, for the borrowing country fits them into its own social context, and something therefore changes. The historical and social conditions of Africa are different from those of Europe, and the political institutions which African countries will find most suitable to express democratic values may well be different. No one can dispute the right of Africans to evolve institutions which fit them best in their own historical and social context. But others have a right to expect the values of democracy to which the institutions give expression to be recognizable. The democratic institutions of France, Britain, and America, for example, have notable differences reflecting the history and social conditions of each country, but underlying them are perceptible values of democracy which they all share. In the same way, India has institutions reflecting Indian history and social structures, but there are recognizable values which she shares with the other democratic countries, and by which they are all judged. Since democracy expresses both principles and ideals, every country will be found to fall short in some respect or other. There are glaringly undemocratic practices in Africa also; we have already had evidence of this, and more appear in later chapters. Good reasons may be given to explain some of the shortcomings, and it helps to promote international harmony for different countries to try to understand one another's problems. But it does not help Africa not to see her shortcomings for what they are, measured against the standards we have seen her leaders to avow. One of the sources of hope for world peace lies in the fact that democracy has a moral language which peoples of different cultures and races can understand. The democratic principle of racial equality has a moral foundation in the shared ideals of democracy. In so far as any country, wherever it may be, professes democracy, there should be common standards by which it can be judged. The countries of Africa which avow democratic ideals—justifiably claim the right to evolve their own institutions; but they may not claim with equal justification to have their own particular brands of democracy with values so different from those of other nations that there are no meeting points. As we have seen, leading spokesmen have not in fact made such a claim. That way, it would appear, lies Babel, and not international understanding or world peace, or evidence of racial equality or common humanity. It is possible for different countries to share the same ideals of democracy, and to aspire towards them, but be at different points of achievement with regard to the expression or realization of democratic values in particular social conditions. But all must submit to judgment by the same values. This is one of the conditions of mutual respect and equality.

CHAPTER SEVEN

Tribalism

One of Africa's most intractable problems is how to integrate different tribes into a modern nation within a democratic framework. All African States have this problem, though its dimensions and urgency vary from State to State.

As we noted in the second chapter, a tribe derives its strength from the sense of belonging which gives a feeling of security to all its members. It consists of kinship groups inhabiting a common territory, possessing a common language and culture, knit together not only by their tradition of common descent, but also by their participation in religious and social activities centred on common interests and values. The solidarity of the tribe has deep foundations.

Tribes vary in size and in political organization. Some consist of a few extended families inhabiting a few dwellings, while others consist of groups of lineages, inhabiting a village, a district, or a large region spread over thousands of square miles. We have noted that the tribes described in *African Political Systems* were divided into two categories on the basis of their political organization: those which lack 'centralized authority, administrative machinery and judicial institutions' and those which possess them.[1]

Some anthropological studies distinguish two types in the first category: (1) the 'simple acephalous' tribe of extended families or villages based on social structures which recognize bilateral kinship,[2] examples of which are the Mende of Sierra Leone, and the Ibo of Nigeria, and (2) the 'acephalous segmentary' tribe which consists of localized, unilinear lineages or clans, each segment of which inhabits a territory of its own, and possesses a political organization independent of the other segments, though several segments may meet on certain ceremonial occasions. The Tallensi of Ghana, and the Nuer of Southern Sudan described in *African Political Systems* are examples of this type. The Banyakole of Uganda and the Ngwato of Bechuanaland described in the same book, are examples of the second category, those that possess government. These different types pose different problems for the building of modern nations. Small tribes which have no traditions of centralized authority pose different problems from large tribes which have developed political institutions and a common heritage and consciousness of belonging together, such as the Yoruba of Nigeria, the Ashanti of Ghana, or the Baganda of Uganda.

There are tribal pressures and tensions in all African States; in the Congo, in Burundi, in Rwanda, and in the Sudan, for example, the tensions have erupted into civil war, murders, and massacre. It has been admitted that tribal cleavages contributed to the events of January 1966 which have resulted in the military takeover of the administration of the Federation of Nigeria where the first pronouncements of the new military régime seem to adumbrate the abolition of the federal structure. In a broadcast to the nation on January 28th, 1966, General Ironsi, the head of the military government said: 'All Nigerians want an end to regionalism. Tribal loyalties and activities which promote tribal consciousness and sectional interests must give way to the urgent task of national reconstruction.'³ Subsequent events, including his murder, have shown that Ironsi underestimated the strength both of tribal feeling and sentiment for some kind of loose federation.

The Nigerian experience affords a good illustration of the general problem of tribalism. Before the country became independent, there were discussions and commissions, and two Constitutional Conferences in London at which questions involving the different ethnic groups loomed large in the minds of the participants. After the first Constitution Conference held in London in May and June 1957, A Special Commission under the chairmanship of Sir Henry Willink was appointed 'to inquire into the fears of minorities and the means of allaying them'. The second Constitutional Conference held in London in September and October 1958 was attended by some 108 Nigerian delegates, representing the three major political parties and their allies. They agreed that only a Federation would enable the different tribes and ethnic groups to be held together in one State. The federal Constitution was at first based on three Regions, North, East, and West; but a fourth, the Mid-West, was created after independence.

The population of Nigeria is put at 55 millions. There are some 248 distinct languages spoken by the different ethnic groups spread over its 373,000 square miles. The Regions of the Federation reflect the heterogeneous ethnic composition. The most ethnically homogeneous is the Western Region which, apart from the few Endo-speaking peoples of the Ondo province, is predominantly Yoruba. The Mid-West Region consists of Endo-speaking peoples, and Jekris, Ijaws, and Ibos. The largest of the tribes in the Eastern Region are Ibos, but there are also Ibibios, Efiks, Ijaws, and small ethnic groups in the Ogoja province. In the Northern Region, the largest, the Fulani, the Hausa, the Kanuri, and the Nupe account for about 60 per cent of the population of the Region; the other tribes are the Tiv, the Birom, the Gwari, and some two hundred small ethnic groups each speaking a different language. To the complexity of ethnic groups have been added differences of religion, education, and economic development. The Fulani, Hausa, Kanuri, and Nupe tribes of the North are Moslem, sharing the Islamic culture; in the rest of the Region, as well as in the South, the Christians or adherents of traditional religions predominate. The South is ahead of the North in education, and economic development, and there are consequently wide differences between North and South.

There are also differences in the political organization of the different ethnic groups. In the North, the Hausa–Fulani conquest of the nineteenth century provided a paternalistic, authoritarian rule of Emirs which continued under the British policy of Indirect Rule. In the West, the Yoruba developed a system of chieftaincy which had delicate checks and balances. Though the large Yoruba Kingdom had split into four chiefdoms by the end of the eighteenth century, and there have been wars between them, the consciousness of a common heritage and of a common ethnic origin provided a sentiment of fraternity among all the Yoruba communities. The Ibos of the East were divided into 30 subtribes, 69 clans, and 500 autonomous villages, which acknowledged no particular political head; but as Dr. Dike noted: 'Beneath the apparent fragmentation of authority lay deep fundamental unities, not only in the religious and cultural spheres but also in matters of politics and economics.'[4]

The Federal structure was designed as a means of containing the minority groups, and of ensuring that the dominant ethnic groups, the Hausa–Fulani in the North, the Yoruba in the West, and the Ibo in the East would co-operate towards national unity and the creation of a stable State. The idea of a federation was carefully examined before it was accepted. But the inherent tribal tensions have persisted. Each of the three major political parties had a regional base which was also tribal, and party strength and rivalries tended to rely on the regional, tribal loyalties. This has had unifying as well as divisive consequences.

The problem posed by the existence of different tribes and ethnic groups in different African States must be approached in the context of what a nation is or is expected to be. Some tend to think of the nation in terms of

the ideal model of a nation towards which the European precedents pointed, even though no such nation existed in total purity, (which) is a single people, traditionally fixed on a well-defined territory, speaking the same language and preferably a language of its own, and shaped to a common mould by many generations of shared historical experience.[5]

Accordingly, they aim at the creation of a nation in which differences of tribe, language, religion, economic development and education, and loyalties to all smaller groups, give place to loyalty to the nation as the only desirable expression of unity.

The new 'African States were created by European Powers who brought together under one administration heterogenous ethnic groups, speaking different languages, sometimes possessing distinct cultures and religions. There are States in which the component tribes have memories of traditional animosities and tribal wars. Added to these are differences in social, economic, and political development which in most States have caused wide regional variations in standards of living and degrees of modernization. We have noted this of Nigeria. It is a common feature of social change in Africa. Aristide Zollberg has noted it in his study of the Ivory Coast. He records that

differentiations between traditional societies have been intensified by the cumulative effect of uneven Western impact, and in recent years, by differential rates of cultural and economic change.... Today the Agni or the Aboure are different from the Bete or the Gouro not only because they eat different foods, speak differently, or settle their disputes according to different norms but because they are wealthier, more educated, and more christian. The Malinke and the Senufo in the past were of two different northern civilizations, but now the Malinke are also more likely to be Moslems, traders, and urbanites, while the Senufo are subsistence farmers and continue to practise their traditional religion.[6]

In situations such as these, it would be visionary to conceive of a nation as one people, speaking a common language, bound together by a common heritage and a shared historical experience. Africa must break loose from this alluring European model. It does not fit in with the social realities of the continent; even in Europe the model applies only to countries like England and France, where it is the product of unique and long histories.

The African situation, in its contemporary context, calls for the concept of a nation of different tribes, possessing a diversity of traditions and even cultures, inhabiting a common territory, bound together by the common desire to preserve their newly won independence and unity, and by the goals of economic, social, cultural, and political progress which they share in common, and which they see can be realized only if they stay together as a nation. There is plenty here on which a stable, democratic society can be built. It is in such realistic terms that the problem of tribalism should be approached.

There are some who think that tribalism should be eradicated by repression and coercion, on the grounds that it obstructs national unity. But coercion violates the democratic principle of government by consent. Repression only leads to instability. Quite apart from this, the forms which tribalism has taken in new social settings give warning that it is too resilient a social force to be dealt with in this way. In a social survey of Sekondi-Takoradi (Ghana) undertaken in 1947–8, the author noted that intense tribal loyalties were manifested in the many tribal associations which existed in the town. Even those who had been town-dwellers for many years showed strong loyalty to their tribe and home village. But 'tribal associations, through the control they exercise over members, are potent factors for law and order, and in this sense form part of the governmental institutions of the municipality'.[7]

Fifteen years or so later Philip Foster, carrying out a study on education and social change in Ghana, noted that

a considerable body of evidence points to the persistence of elements of traditional social structure even within the most 'modern' sectors of Ghanaian society. Ethnic background, kinship affiliation, and traditional residence patterns still play a role even within the urban context and indeed may provide the basis for organizations which appear at first sight to be essentially Western in nature. For example, voluntary self-help associations, trade unions, and political parties all contain components based upon traditional patterns of association and affiliation.[8]

The growth of ethnic associations is a feature that has been noted throughout Africa.[9] We choose Zollberg's study of the Ivory Coast for another illustration, because of the insight it affords of how tribalism ties in with politics. Zollberg observed that traditional ties remained extremely important, and that most towns in the Ivory Coast were divided into ethnically distinct neighbourhoods. Also,

a major phenomenon in the new towns during the inter-war period was the rise of ethnic associations. These groups, whatever name they are called, have in common an organization based on traditional social groupings—the lineage, the clan, the village-group or the tribe.[10]

Zollberg quotes from a speech by A. Denise, then Prime Minister, expressing his concern about this development during the Constitutional debates of 1959:

We are not a territory fortunate enough but to have a limited number of ethnic groups. We have more than 62 tribes and, during the 10 or 13 years since the Ivory Coast was born to political life, we have had as our ambition in the midst of a party all of you know well and in which the majority of us are militants, we thought that we might arrive at a fusion of these tribes, in order that little by little a sort of single race might emerge. Instead of this, we see the opposite and there is a proliferation of societies that do nothing but separate the population into ethnic and tribal components.[11]

One of the officials of the Prime Minister's party explained to Zollberg how they had come to terms with the situation:

During the elections (of 1945 and 1946) we had found that the ethnic associations that existed in the city (Abidjan) functioned effectively for election purposes as well. . . . Regardless of where they lived and worked in the city, people of the same tribe came together for social purposes. So we transformed the ethnic associations into party sub-committees. Where they did not exist, we helped the tribes to organize original ones. Only in this way could we communicate with the members, collect dues, and pass down party directives in the various local languages.[12]

An explanation reported to have been given by A. Denise is illuminating. He was then proposing to table a government motion to abolish the ethnic groups because 'all these associations are engaged in a constant struggle for different political views, even though they claim to be absolutely apolitical'.[13] Zollberg concludes, 'It is therefore because tradition is a source of pluralism that it must be combated.'

As we see it, the social realities suggest that a sounder approach to the problem of tribalism in Africa is to accept the fact of pluralism, rather than fly in the face of the facts and attempt to achieve monolithic structures through coercion. It is no sign of backwardness to recognize the fact of the existence of different tribes and ethnic groups, nor is it reactionary to seek accommodation with tribal loyalties. Ethnic groups exist everywhere in the world.

In their survey of political trends in the new nations of Africa and Asia, Almond and Coleman had this to say:

Although the racial and tribal pluralism of the new political communities tends to retard the process of national unification, it is not a barrier to their survival, nor is it necessarily unhealthy

I

in terms of the development of competitive societies. The multiplicity of tribes within a state is not everywhere an obstacle to the creation of a broader political nationality. Indeed, the larger their number and the smaller their size, the better are the chances of effective amalgamation. Moreover, it could be argued that such a rich pluralism makes dictatorship less likely by providing countervailing power centres which cannot be coerced into a single authoritarian system.[14]

This view is well-founded and merits attention. The growth of ethnic associations is not necessarily incompatible with the building of a democratic nation. It may even afford better prospects for democracy, in consonance both with group interest and the preservation of civic liberties against the encroachment of dictatorship.

The problem of tribalism is essentially a problem of regional development and local government, for most tribes are still territorial units. Under colonial rule, as we have noted, the people were divorced from participation in local affairs. They were not afforded enough opportunities in sharing in the decisions and policies which affected their own lives. Where there are ethnic groups that had a tradition of self-government and consciousness of a common heritage before the colonial era, they will, at independence, want to manage their own affairs, and will only feel themselves a part of the wider nation if they are able to do so. But in the early days of independence, the desire for national unity becomes so paramount, and the tendency towards centralization so strong that any groups that want to defend local liberties are regarded as disruptive.

Accommodation with territorial tribal units implies decentralization and devolution. There are traditional precedents for the devolution of power from the centre to

component units. We have pointed out that decentralization marked the Ashanti political system. In the plural
societies of the new States, it is necessary that people should
have opportunities to look after their own affairs as far as
they are able to do so. The problem becomes one of what
local authorities to create, and how to divide functions between central authorities and local authorities. Each State
will have to face its own problem of devolution in its own
social context. A democratic nation is strengthened by a
foundation of local democracy.

Some see decentralization as yielding to separatism, and
so they advocate measures that tend to increasing centralization and authoritarianism; while others see it as a means
whereby tribes of diverse traditions, and sometimes of wide
regional differences, can be kept together to preserve the
nation from breaking apart. It is at the level of regional and
local government that there is the strongest case for the development of political institutions that must meet the particular historical and social realities of African States; yet it
is at those levels that there are the most conspicuous
examples of efforts to copy irrelevant models from Britain
and France. Tribalism, whether it is manifested by an ethnic group large enough to be a region, or only by a small
one occupying a village, offers opportunities for ventures in
local self-government, and for strengthening the base of
democracy by developing political institutions which enable
all the groups to manage their own affairs within their respective competences, and contribute to the larger unit of
the nation. If the regions of a State are more evenly developed, and the people are able to share adequately in the
government of their own areas, tribalism will cease to be a
divisive force. People will not cease to be members of their

tribes, or to cherish that membership; but they can also be members of the State, along with fellow citizens who are members of other tribes, and share with them a sense of belonging together, and cherish their citizenship, because it makes them members of a wider society.

CHAPTER EIGHT

Democracy and One-party Systems

Single-party regimes are now in vogue in Africa. They have been achieved through various ways in the different countries, by mergers, dissolution, absorption, or suppression of opposition parties. As far as West Africa is concerned, Professor Arthur Lewis finds 'it significant that no party now in power went to the polls in a free election seeking a mandate to create a single-party system. . . . Single-party power was seized, not granted by the voters.'[1] He examines the different reasons given to justify the system, and finds that the single-party

fails in all its claims. It cannot represent all the people; or maintain free discussion; or give stable government; or, above all, reconcile the differences between various regional groups. . . . It is partly the product of the hysteria of the moment of independence, when some men found it possible to seize the State and suppress their opponents. It is a disease from which West Africa deserves to recover.[2]

Though these conclusions are based on a reasoned examination of the facts, the progressive adoption of the single-party by one African country after another attests to its popularity with African leaders.

The latest in the queue is Sierra Leone where the Prime Minister, Sir Albert Margai, has told his people (January 1966) that he favours a single-party State, because the multi-party system has caused dissensions, whereas in Ghana, the 'people speak with one mind, since the introduction of the one-party', which, as he sees it, is 'the way to salvation for Sierra Leone'. A Commission is therefore to be set up to consider the matter. Strong opposition has already come from Freetown, the capital, but the Prime Minister says Freetown does not represent opinion in the rest of the country. The Prime Minister's reported speech is reminiscent of what Kruschev told the Indian Parliament on his visit to India in 1960.

The Soviet society is a society of working men, peasants, and intellectuals with their roots in the people, united by a community of interests and a singleness of purpose. The interests of the Soviet people are expressed and upheld by one party—the Communist Party.... This is what accounts for the absence of any other parties in our country.[3]

Among the arguments advanced to justify the system is that it promotes democracy, and this is the aspect we must examine.

To illustrate how one-party régimes have been formed, we may cite the cases of three States where there have been military coups recently, Dahomey, the Central African Republic, and Upper Volta.

There was a military seizure of power in Dahomey on December 22nd, 1965, led by General Soglo. It was his third intervention since 1963. Like most of the newly independent States, Dahomey started with more than one party. At elections held in April 1959, three parties won seats in the national Legislature: the Parti Republicain de Dahomey (PRD), which won 28 seats, the Rassemblement Democratique Dahomeen (RDD) 22 seats, and the Union Democratique Dahomeenne (UDD) 20 seats. After the elections of 1959, the PRD and the RDD who had been allies combined to form the Parti Dahomeen de l'Unite (PDU) to fight the elections of 1960 which it won against the UDD. A year later, the PDU government dissolved the UDD, and arrested many of its members, including its leader. The PDU then absorbed the remaining opposition parties. Party squabbles, however, have continued.

In the Central African Republic where Colonel Bokassa ousted President Dacko on January 1st, 1966, there were previously two parties, the Mouvement pour l'évolution Sociale de l'Afrique noire (MESAN), and the Mouvement pour l'évolution Démocratique en Afrique Centrale (MEDAC) which contested elections held in September 1960. MESAN won by 32 seats, against 11 by MEDAC. In February the following year, the MESAN government dissolved the MEDAC opposition party, and arrested some of its members.

Colonel Lamizana, Chief of Staff, deposed President Yameogo on January 4th, 1966, and set up a military government in Upper Volta. In elections held in April 1959 the Union Démocratique Voltaique (UDV) won 64 seats, and the Parti du Regroupment Africain (PRA) 11 seats. The PRA was succeeded in opposition by two other parties, the Parti National Voltaique and the Parti Republicain de la Liberté, but they were both dissolved by the UDV government. Some of the opposition leaders left the country, and others were placed in administrative internment.

The single-party régimes of Africa all claim to be democratic, but in practice their adherence to democratic values shows wide variations which may be illustrated by comparing Ghana with Tanzania.*

At the last elections held in Ghana in 1956, the Convention People's Party (CPP) won 177 seats, the National Liberation Movement (NLM) 12 seats, the Northern People's Party (NPP) 15 seats, and the Togoland Congress and others 6 seats. In 1957 the Opposition parties amalgamated to form the United Party. By 1962, with some opposition members crossing the floor, others detained and unseated, there were only 8 members in the opposition in the National Assembly which then numbered 114, the 1960 Republican Constitution having provided for the addition of 10 women members. In September 1962 a motion was passed in the National Assembly for the establishment of a single-party State.

This was one of the issues subsequently presented to the people to vote upon in a referendum in January 1964. The published official figures claimed that 93.69 per cent of the registered voters had gone to the polls, and that 92.81 per cent voted in favour of the proposal to set up a one-party State. Foreign journalists who were in Ghana to observe the elections told a different story. Among them were two correspondents of *The Guardian* who were invited as observers. They reported that behind the published figures lay 'a mixture of intimidation and ballot-rigging which ranged from the farcical to the brutal'.[4] They reported that voters were warned that anyone who voted 'NO' would be found out and punished. This could be done because each voter's ballot paper had a serial number which appeared against his name in the electoral register. During the actual voting,

* The name under which Tanganyika united with Zanzibar.

in some of the polling booths, the slots of the 'no' boxes were sealed, some late voters were given extra ballot papers to put in the 'yes' boxes; in other polling booths, voters had to drop their ballot papers into the 'yes' boxes while the Polling Officers looked on. The observers found that 'it was apparent from this blend of falsification and coercion that the party had told its key officials from district to district to find their own way to the agreed end'. In a broadcast to the nation on February 5th, 1964, after the referendum, President Nkrumah said ominously that they had reached a stage that 'demands that everyone within our society must either accept the spirit and aims of our revolution or expose themselves as the deceivers and betrayers of the people'. One of the proposals that had been submitted to the people at the referendum was that the President should be empowered to dismiss judges of the Superior Courts 'for reasons which appear to him sufficient'. In March 1964 the President dismissed three judges from the Supreme Court, and one from the High Court.

That the uttered threats were not empty can be judged from Ghana's Preventive Detention Act and the use to which it has been put. The Preventive Detention Bill was introduced into Parliament on July 14th, 1958, and it received the Governor-General's assent on July 18th, 1958. Since then it has been the principal instrument for stifling opposition to the government. It was required by the Act that the list of those detained under the law should be published in the Government Gazette, and this was done for a while. In November 1958, 43 persons, most of them members of the United Party were arrested and detained under the Act; some of them are still in prison, eight years later, without trial. On December 23rd, 1960, 118 persons were also taken into preventive detention; on October 3rd, 1961, among 50 persons who were arrested and detained were Mr. J. E. Appiah, Deputy Leader of the Opposition, and Dr. J. B. Danquah, one of the most prominent political leaders in the country, a leading member of the opposition, and a Presidential candidate who stood against Dr. Nkrumah for the Presidency. Dr. Danquah was released after ten months, then was re-arrested and detained until his death in prison after thirteen months, on February 4th, 1965, at the age of seventy. Dr. Nnamdi Azikiwe, then President of Nigeria, said in a tribute to his memory:

> I am sorry that Dr. Danquah died in a detention camp. I am of the considered opinion that if independence means the substitution of indigenous tyranny for alien rule, then those who struggled for the independence of former colonial territories have not only desecrated the cause of human freedom but have betrayed their people. I wish Dr. Danquah had been tried publicly, told what offence he was alleged to have committed, given a fair opportunity to defend himself, and then either discharged or punished, depending upon the fact whether or not his innocence had been established or his guilt proved beyond any reasonable shadow of doubt.

There are many others, young men and old, known to have died while in detention.

The arrests and detentions under the Act have continued, but it is not known exactly how many are in detention because the requirement to publish the list of detainees in the official Gazette has long been discontinued. From unofficial sources, the number is believed to have stood above 1,000 since 1961. On November 6th, 1963, the re-enactment of the Preventive Detention Act of 1958 empowered the continued detention, for a further five years, of many who had already been in prison since 1958; and the Preventive Detention Act of 1964 has empowered the President to make restriction orders against any Ghanaian if he is of the opinion that Preventive Detention would be unsuitable 'on account of age or health or for any other reason'. The International Commission of Jurists has commented:

It is impossible to see respect for human rights and the Rule of Law when a man may be detained for ten years without ever being accused of any crime, let alone being tried and convicted.[5]

In an authentic letter dated February 20th, 1965, addressed to the Right Honourable Harold Wilson, Prime Minister of Great Britain, smuggled out of a detention prison in Accra, the writers gave an eye-opening and informative account of the use of the Preventive Detention Act. The opening paragraphs of the letter may be quoted:

Mr. Prime Minister,

We, helpless detainees of this prison, have the honour to present to you our humble congratulations on the election of your Party to the Government of Great Britain, and of yourself to its premiership. We also take this opportunity to draw your attention to our sad and distressing state, to appeal to you and through you to the 700 million peoples and their several governments of the Commonwealth to come to our aid so as to secure for us release from what appears virtual imprisonment for life for no other 'crime' than that of political opposition and the fact that the core of us do not share the clear neo-communist ideas of President Kwame Nkrumah and his associates.

None of us has been convicted of any crime, yet many of us have already completed close on 7, 6, 5, 4 or 3 years of imprisonment, as the case may be, in conditions of severity worse than those laid down by law and accorded to convict prisoners. Nearly every prison in Ghana has its quota of detainees, but this prison is the chief concentration centre. Here we number nearly 600:

(a) Members of Parliament and other leading figures and supporters of the party in opposition to Nkrumah's party at independence and subsequently brought together in the United Party of Ghana; their arrests began in November 1958 in an atmosphere of great calmness in the country but generally accompanied by specious allegations of activities prejudicial to the security of the State.

(b) So-called Criminal Detainees arrested in the later months of 1960 (following a ghastly crime of robbery with violence and murder in Accra), they are mostly persons of known criminal records and others suspected of criminal activities but some of whom have in fact never been convicted previously.

(c) A number of CPP members and supporters previously used by government and party leaders for shady activities (including criminal ones), frauds and extortions, their detentions were arranged by their principals to prevent the leakage of those activities as the persons became disgruntled.

(d) Personal enemies of government party leaders, regional and district commissioners who exercise the power of submitting names of persons to be detained.

(e) A body of paid government party workers—the 'Propaganda Unit' of the CPP Headquarters detained in 1962 because they are suspected of being supporters or sympathisers of their fallen party leaders Tawiah Adamafio, Ako Adjei and Kofi Crabbe.

(f) A number of very highly-placed police officers dismissed and later detained following an attempt to shoot President Nkrumah by a junior police officer in January 1964.

(g) Other persons detained upon spiteful but false reports made against them by personal enemies who happen to know what to say to get a person imprisoned under the Preventive Detention Act without inquiry, including persons detained so that their wives might become available for interested suitors, or their properties misappropriated by false claimants or their businesses destroyed.

There is a large number of persons unclassified. For some time now the government has dispensed with the statutory formality of giving to persons detained grounds of detention within five days as provided by the law. Quite logical since the Ghana Courts, under the leadership of Chief Justice Sir Arku Korsah—a registered member of the CPP—have abdicated their power of protecting Ghanaian citizens against imprisonment on trumped charges by conducting the trial called for under Habeas Corpus applications. So persons are merely removed from their homes and sent into the prisons without being given any information whatever as to the reason for the action against them.

There are young men among us who have already spent fully one quarter of their lives in prison since their detention in 1958, and there are very old men—well over 80—who, in their senile decay, hardly know what it is all about.

The petitioners then went on to give accounts of ill-treatment and even torture of political detainees. The Ghana Government refused the allegations and announced that various bodies would be invited to inspect the prisons and report their findings, but this was not done. The petitioners stated in the letter that 'the Supreme Court of Ghana has bound us hand and foot and gagged us and then delivered us and the people of Ghana to the tender mercies of Kwame Nkrumah and his associates'. This is so, because

(a) the Ghana Preventive Detention Act empowers the President, solely in his discretion, to deprive any subject of his liberty, virtually for life;

(b) the Ghana Courts have held that the discretion is absolute;

(*c*) the President in the exercise of this absolute discretion is not answerable to Parliament, or any court or tribunal;

(*d*) the person detained is denied the elementary, natural justice of facing his accusers or putting his case;

(*e*) there is no provision or protection whatsoever against the indiscriminate abuse of the powers conferred by the Act.

In 1961 the International Commission of Jurists published a study of Ghana's Preventive Detention Act. Their concluding observations were as follows:

Without going into the political questions as to whether there existed or exists in Ghana a situation calling for legislation providing for preventive detention, it is apparent that there are certain factors in connection with the Ghana Act which, from a legal point of view, are not satisfactory.

(i) The maximum duration of the preventive detention seems long especially when it is taken into account that there is no indication that the term of detention comes up for regular review by the executive as it does, for example, in Southern Rhodesia, and in view also of the recommendation of Commission II of the African Conference on the Rule of Law quoted above.

(ii) On account of the inability of the detainee to face his accusers and put his case there appears to be an infringement of a rule of natural justice; written representations, it is submitted, are not enough.

(iii) There is no independent tribunal before whom the detainee can make his objection.

(iv) Those persons detained give the appearance certainly of being drawn very considerably from one political party.

(v) If the Akoto and Vanderpuye (two of the detainees) cases are typically illustrative, the specific details filed on the grounds of detention appear inadequate.

(vi) Because of the narrow subjective interpretation of the words 'if satisfied', the Courts have precluded themselves from investigating the grounds of the President's satisfaction. Judicial review, therefore, does not seem to have provided in Ghana a strong safeguard for the liberty of the subject.[6]

From the account we have given of the re-enactments and further use of the Act since this study by the International Commission of Jurists was published over four years ago, it will be seen that the safeguards of the liberty of the subject have been further eroded by the extension of the control of the President over both Parliament and the Judiciary and by the perpetual use of the weapon of imprisonment without trial. The one-party régime in Ghana has meant the concentration of power over all the organs of State in the hands of one man. The foundations of democracy have been undermined.

A part of this process has been government and party control of the press as well as broadcasting. There is no independent paper in Ghana, and both press and radio only tell the people what the government wants them to know. There is also a censorship of news sent abroad by foreign correspondents. A further curtailment of freedom has been foreshadowed. In November 1964 the government set up a Committee of nine persons to 'work out a system to ensure the removal of all publications which do not reflect the ideology of the party or are antagonistic to its ideas'. Free access to information and knowledge appear to be in danger.

In March 1965 the Vice-Chancellor of the University of Ghana, Dr. Conor Cruise O'Brien, in an address at the university stated that 'there are clear signs that influential elements in the community wish to turn the university from a centre of critical and independent thought into something quite different, and that they are making some progress in the direction they desire'. During the preceding year, six members of the university teaching staff, four American, one West Indian, and one British, had been dismissed and deported; the President and officers of the Ghana Students Union had been arrested and detained for protesting against the dismissal of the Chief Justice; party members had been sent to the university to stage demonstrations during which they damaged university property, and it had been announced by the government that scholarships held at universities in Ghana would be reviewed annually 'on the basis of satisfactory performance and good conduct', and the *Ghanaian Times*, a mouthpiece of the CPP, explained that this meant 'close identification with the spirit and objects of the party'. It can be seen that the single-party régime in Ghana does not mean a strengthening of democracy, but rather its replacement with a dictatorship.

The Tanzanian experiment differs at several points from the Ghanaian version. The Tanganyika African National Union (TANU), the ruling party, already had overwhelming support, before its National Executive Committee resolved in January 1963 that Tanganyika should become a single-party State. Many of the party's candidates were sure to be returned unopposed both in national and local elections.

A Presidential Commission was set up in February 1964 to suggest changes which should be made in the Constitution of Tanganyika in order to establish a 'democratic one-party State'. In its Report, the Commission stated that its terms were 'to devise new constitutional forms which will enable the ordinary man to participate more fully in the process of government',[7] and 'to adjust the institutions of the one-party system in government, to permit wider democratic participation and fuller discussion of national issues'.[8]

The Commission commented on the effect which the dominant position of the party and the return of so many of its members to parliament unopposed had had on debates in the National Assembly:

> With a few notable exceptions debates in the National Assembly have tended to be lifeless and superficial. Legislation of the most complex and far-reaching kind has passed rapidly through all its stages without challenge to basic principles or careful examination of detailed provisions.[9]

This was one of the developments to be corrected. Another was that the return of so many candidates unopposed had in fact robbed the electorate of the opportunity of choosing its representatives.

Although the overwhelming support which TANU commanded had made Tanganyika virtually a one-party State, the proposal to make it one by law did not go unchallenged. There was a small opposition party, an amalgamation of the African National Congress and the People's Democratic Party which was under the leadership of Christopher Tumbo, a former Tanganyika High Commissioner in London. The opposition party claimed to have suffered various forms of persecution to hamper its progress: restrictions on its freedom to organize meetings, vexatious prosecutions of its members, and difficulties put in its way regarding the registration of its district branches.

K

as the law required. After the National Executive of TANU had taken the decision in January 1963 that Tanganyika should become a one-party State, the opposition party was dissolved. Tumbo left to live in Kenya in exile, and tried to organize a new party from there. In February 1964 the Kenya authorities arrested him and returned him to Tanganyika where he was detained under the Tanganyika Preventive Detention Act. He has since been in prison.

Tumbo had opposed the Preventive Detention Act which was passed in September 1962. The Act empowers the Minister for Home Affairs to detain anyone at any time, whether there is a State of Emergency or not, and for any period of time, subject only to an annual review by an Advisory Committee whose advice the Minister is not obliged to accept. According to section 3 of the Act, the Minister's decision that a preventive detention order should be issued may not be questioned in any court. This background to the establishment of the one-party State is noteworthy.

By notices in the *Tanganyika Gazette* in February 1964, the public were invited to submit memoranda to the Commission on the Constitution. Among the memoranda submitted was one by the President of the Tanganyika Law Society. It dealt mainly with civil liberties and the Rule of Law, as the following excerpts show:

Fundamental human rights are not peculiar to any particular political system, country, race or community. They are something basic. All human beings in whatever country desire to lead peaceful well-settled lives and the Government must respect this desire and to this extent the Government must limit its power. 'The theory of fundamental rights implies limited

Government. It aims at preventing the Government and legislature from becoming totalitarian, and in doing so it affords the individual an opportunity for self-development.' By incorporating these rights in the Constitution we ensure their strict enforcement.

We regard the following as fundamental and inalienable rights of Mankind:

1. The Right to Life.
2. Freedom from Inhuman Treatment.
3. Freedom from Slavery.
4. The Right to Liberty.
5. Cultural and Educational Rights.
6. The Right to Property.
7. Freedom of Expression.
8. Freedom of Peaceful Assembly and Association.
9. Freedom from Discriminatory Legislation.
10. Freedom of Worship.

A provision should be incorporated in the Constitution stating that all laws which are repugnant to or inconsistent with or take away or abridge the fundamental rights are null and void.

The second cardinal principle of the Rule of Law is the irremovability of the Judiciary who must guarantee security of tenure until death or retirement at an age fixed by statute. Safeguards must be provided against the arbitrary removal of judges. Such removal should only take place under exceptional circumstances and then only after the matter has been lawfully considered by a body of judicial character.

The High Court must have unfettered power to safeguard and enforce the rights guaranteed under the Constitution. To this end, the particular remedies such as the writs of habeas corpus, certiorari and mandamus, etc., available under all democratic legal systems should also be available here.

The Report of the Commission was published in April 1965. The new Constitution based on its recommendations was passed by the National Assembly in July, and Parliamentary and Presidential elections based on the new Constitution were held in October 1965.

For our study of democracy, several points of the Commission's recommendations should be noted. The Commission assigns the formulation of policy to the National Executive Committee of TANU, while the National Assembly is 'primarily concerned with the more detailed task of giving effect to government policy through appropriate legislative measures and exercising vigilant control over all aspects of government expenditure'.[10] All members of the National Assembly must be members of TANU. The Commission stated: 'Our conception of TANU as a National Political Movement carries with it the implication that all organized political activity must take place within the framework of the Party itself.'[11]

In order to give electors the opportunity of choosing candidates, the Commission proposed that two candidates should stand for election in each constituency. Every nomination should be supported by twenty-five registered voters. The nominations should first go before the TANU District Conference of the Constituency where three candidates will be selected for each constituency from the nominations. The final selection of the two candidates to stand for election in each constituency is made by the National Executive. After this final selection, it is the responsibility of the District Executive Committee of the party to plan the election campaign for the candidates.

As regards individual rights, the Commission said they had 'constantly in mind the need to ensure that any new arrangements we propose will not unnecessarily encroach on the freedom of the individual',[12] but they could not recommend the incorporation of a Bill of Rights in the Constitution because

Discussions concerning the extent to which individual rights must give way to wider considerations of social progress are not properly judicial decisions. They are political decisions best taken by political leaders responsible to the electorate.[13]

They therefore wished to avoid conflict:

the maintenance of the Rule of Law to which we attach the greatest importance requires particular care that occasions for conflict between Judges and the Executive and the Legislature should be reduced to the minimum.[14]

In place of a Bill of Rights, the Commission recommended an alternative 'which will not have the effect of limiting the actions of the Government and Party in a way which could hinder the task of nation building'. The alternative was that the new Constitution should provide for the appointment by the President of a permanent Commission with a wide jurisdiction to inquire into allegations of abuse of power by government and party officials. Such a Commission should be enabled to tour the Regions, and it should be empowered to summon witnesses and call for papers, including official papers in the custody of officers of the government.

While it is evident that the Tanzanian one-party experiment shows concern both for the Rule of Law and for the rights of the individual, limitations inherent in the system are also manifest. It provides for choice, so long as this is within the limits of the party and its policies and programmes. The electorate can only vote for candidates of the one party; they therefore can choose persons, but there is not a choice of policies or programmes or leadership. In the recent elections, the Minister of Finance was among the candidates who lost their seats. Was it because he was personally disliked, or did the voters thereby express disapproval of the policies he sought to implement? Those policies were not personal to him. He was carrying out the policies of the party. These, however, could not be changed by his defeat at the polls.

Members of the party can criticize and express opinions within the party, but it may be asked to what extent the party can accommodate ideologies that conflict with its own, or tolerate ideas which do not fall within its own presuppositions and philosophy? Will such dissenters find themselves in detention? The Preventive Detention Act has provided for this, beyond the jurisdiction of the Courts. Broadly, the question involves the extent to which a party that has a particular person as leader, and a definite policy and programme to which all must be loyal can at the same time be an open party which can contain all opinions. What about those who reject the leadership or the policies? Even where there is agreement on objectives, the differences on methods and priorities by which to achieve the objectives can be very important and fundamental. These are some of the questions to which the experimentation with the single-party within the framework of democracy must provide answers.

Every democratic community must have effective checks on its rulers. Democracy rejects the view that the leader, and the group around him who lead the single-party always infallibly seek the interests of the people, or embody the will of all. The leader and the group and all who constitute the party are fallible men and women, on whom there must be effective checks in the exercise of the powers they wield.

This implies the right of the people to oppose, and their right to choose and to change their rulers and leaders. The political institutions must provide democratic outlets for the exercise of these rights.

There appear to be two crucial questions for Africa: the way in which to institutionalize opposition, and how to make it possible to change a single-party government that has failed to satisfy the people. Some single-party devices are in effect self-perpetuating organs for the leaders.

Sir Abubakar Tafewa Balewa, the late Prime Minister of Nigeria, is reported to have said in answer to a question put to him at the last interview he gave to a visiting journalist before his death:

I have told people all along that we are not ripe for a system of government in which there is a full-fledged opposition. In Nigeria, no party can agree to be in opposition for long. A political opposition in the Western accepted sense is a luxury that we cannot afford. You see, today in Parliament—there the MPs are performing, some of them, some of the duties of the Opposition. So they can. Let them criticize; let them condemn this government—let them say anything they like. The trouble is that the Nigerian Member of Parliament wants to criticize the government and to be in it at the same time. Democracy, democracy—what is it? There is American democracy, British democracy—why not Nigerian democracy? I wish we could find that.[15]

They were exploring it in a coalition government, but it seems this did not go far enough. As the main political parties were regionally based, and the Northern Region had a preponderant majority of the seats in the National Assembly, a coalition based on two of the main parties was in fact a combination of the Northern Region and another

Region against the third. No coalition could command a workable majority without the North. This nursed a sense of injustice and frustration at the domination of the comparatively more developed Southern Regions, by the less developed Northern Region. The situation pointed to a coalition government in which all the Regions were represented.

The remark that the Nigerian Member of Parliament wants to criticize the government and at the same time be a member of it is interesting; for the right to criticize a government of which one is a member was one of the built-in checks of the traditional Ashanti political system. The members of the Chief's Council representing different lineages or areas were expected to criticize, and even though the ultimate objective was to reach consensus, there was also the constitutional right of the chief to take steps to destool a member of the Council, and the constitutional right of the members of the Council to destool the chief. Both rights were governed by traditional checks to prevent arbitrary action. It is as though there were arrangements not only for a Prime Minister or President to dismiss a Cabinet Minister, but also for the Cabinet to be able to initiate the deposition of the President or the Prime Minister. In either case, the ultimate power lay with the electors. The right to criticize did not abrogate the right to change the leader. Democratic restraints and discipline were obviously needed for the proper functioning of the system. Further, although there was no permanent opposition as such, the people had rights not only in the election and deposition of their rulers but also to criticize. This right was institutionalized. There were traditional ceremonies at which the people, particularly the women, could lampoon in song and dance against their rulers with impunity. So there were recognized occasions when the chief, in spite of the sacral nature of his office, was reminded that he was just as fallible as other mortals, and he had to listen to his wrongs as they were brought home to him.

It is right that Africa should seek her own institutions, and not pattern her institutions on those of Britain or France or America or Russia or any other country. But the single-party system is not an original or unique African institution. It exists in other parts of the world where its history and achievements can be studied. It is open to question whether it is the best way to ensure the democratic values of freedom, justice, human rights, and the Rule of Law which African States avow. Judged by these accepted standards and values, the records are not reassuring. Even the best examples of the one-party régimes smother some essential democratic rights, and the freedom of associations like trade unions, farmers', women's, youth, traders', and other associations; others are flagrant dictatorships which afford no democratic avenues for change, and, as the records abundantly testify, offer only the alternative of military coups.

CHAPTER NINE

The Search for Union and World Brotherhood

The pace of change in Africa is not only rapid but bewildering; but underneath all the varied events, certain recurrent causes may be discerned; whether, to take some current topics, the events be military coups, or a group of States in Africa agreeing on 'dual nationality', or Rhodesia seizing independence illegally, or refugees from Mozambique straggling over the border into Zambia. These events mark a continent in restless turmoil. The recurrent causes are Africa's search for better standards of living, for wider, more prosperous unions, and for acceptance as equals in the Brotherhood of Man. These themes are traceable through the bewildering kaleidoscope of change and revolution.

The year 1966, as we have seen, opened with military coups: in Central Africa on January 1st, in Upper Volta on the 4th, and, the least expected, in Nigeria on January 15th. It seems a time of political instability. Of the three, Nigeria seemed a very stable State; more than that the country appeared to be making a success of democratic government. The press and the people had successfully resisted the introduction of Preventive Detention, and the citizen of Nigeria was immune from arbitrary arrest and imprisonment; the

Rule of Law prevailed, the Judiciary was independent, and the Nigerian Courts had won international respect; civil liberties were assured in a Bill of Rights entrenched in the Constitution; there was free political discussion, and the Nigerian press was the least controlled in Africa. The gross National output had risen steadily at an annual rate of 4 per cent over the past five years, and Nigeria had attracted foreign investment which averaged 15 per cent of the gross national output. There were serious wrangles over elections, but it was thought they would be solved like previous ones.

The plan of action and of reforms announced by Major-General Ironsi, head of the Federal Military Government, in a broadcast to the nation on January 28th, 1966, reveal the underlying problems. As the following excerpts show, they are problems which afflict other African countries:

The Federal Military Government will stamp out corruption and dishonesty in our public life with ruthless efficiency and restore integrity and self-respect in our public affairs. In the public service, efficiency and merit will be the criteria for advancement. The Government will study very carefully the questions posed by those who recklessly abused their public offices through the acquisition of State lands and financial deals....

The major problems facing us are the rapid development of the Nigerian economy and the problem of unemployment....

In the field of economic development, Nigeria will require foreign capital and technical know-how from abroad. The Government will ensure that such foreign assistance will be properly utilized in the interest of the country....

We also recognize the important role of private investment. To this end the Government is revising the legislation relating to incentives in order to assist genuine private businessmen wishing to establish projects of benefit to the economy.[1]

The lesson revealed here is that a democratic society, for politic as well as moral reasons must fight against poverty, and unfair distribution of the nation's wealth. Large-scale corruption practised by those in public office meant an unfair distribution; some took more than their fair share, and the glaring contrast between their conspicuous consumption, and the penury of the majority was galling. It was a hidden bomb. Other governments in Africa are sitting on similar bombs.

The need for rapid economic development is general. All African countries are faced with the fact that the majority of their peoples live in poverty. What General Ironsi said of Nigeria applies to all African States; they all need outside help for development. Experience has shown that they do not all get what they expect, but they can rely on getting some help, because over the last twenty years, the richer countries have awakened to the needs of the poorer countries in Asia, Africa, and Latin America. That awakening has contributed to the growing consciousness of a world community. The rich countries are increasingly accepting a moral obligation to help the poor. This can be seen in the expanding economic aid from the industrial countries. On May 14th, 1964, Mr. Kruschev, then Prime Minister of the Soviet Union, opened the Aswan dam of the United Arab Republic, built with massive Russian aid. In January 1966 President Nkrumah opened the £57 million Volta Dam built with British and American aid; the smelter which will be the main user of the electric power, and so justify its production, is being financed by private American capital, backed by the United States Government. The United States is providing $225 million in aid to Nigeria towards her Development Plan for the period 1962–8. This includes the $200 million Niger Dam project. All over Africa, there are projects being financed with aid from the industrial countries of both East and West. The Western countries are the major donors. Aid to Africa from them, not including American aid, rose from $906 million in the fiscal year 1956 to $1.1 billion in 1963. France and Britain provided two-thirds of that sum. The European Economic Community has provided more than $100 million annually in aid to African countries associated with the community. For 1965, the AID Programme of the United States provided for $219 million for Africa, more than half of it for four countries: Nigeria, Tunisia, Sudan, and Liberia. We may ask what this new phenomenon of aid from the richer countries to Africa implies. Britain and America have provided their own answers.

During the financial year 1963–4, the British Government's gross bilateral disbursements in grants and loans to Commonwealth countries in Africa, including Nigeria, was £51,828,000. The provisional figure for the 1964–5 financial year was £59,901,000. These loans provide foreign exchange for the purchase of needed imports; but Africa needs not only capital but skilled personnel also—engineers, doctors, teachers, administrators, technicians, and others. These are provided under Technical Assistance, which is aid in the form of skills rather than capital. In the financial year 1963–4, British personnel working in Commonwealth countries in Africa under Technical Assistance services numbered 9,920.

We intend to give the highest priority to technical assistance; this provides skilled men and women to help in development and, above all, in the education and training of local people and it is often a prerequisite for enabling a country to make good use of financial aid[2] [so says an official British publication].

It is not only governments that have become conscious of the embryonic world community, but individual citizens as well. Some of them have felt that they should give practical expression of this realization by volunteering for service overseas. In Britain such service has been given under the auspices of Voluntary Service Overseas, International Voluntary Service, the National Union of Students, and the United Nations Association. The British Government makes contributions to these voluntary bodies: £28,000 in the financial year 1962–3, and £62,000 in the financial year 1964–5. In 1965 there were 900 volunteers overseas, serving under the aegis of the four agencies. Why this concern for Africa, and this desire to help shown by the government, private agencies, and individuals?

Three reasons are discernible in a recent document published by the British Government on overseas development. The first is simply that it is moral for the rich to help the poor.

Our aim is to do what lies in our power to help the developing countries to provide their people with the material opportunities of using their talents, of living a full and happy life, and of steadily improving their lot. The basis of the aid programme is therefore a moral one. ... We must recognize that poverty in a world of growing wealth causes discontent and unrest to which economic and social development is the only possible answer. We must therefore be ready to share our wealth and knowledge so as to help promote the progress and strengthen the stability of the developing countries by increasing the material well-being of their peoples.[3]

The second reason frankly admits that Britain also stands to gain by helping other countries to develop:

The provision of aid is to our long-term economic advantage. We have a special interest in encouraging the expansion of international trade;... By helping to raise incomes in the developing countries we can provide expanding markets for exports and safeguard the supply of our imports and the return on our investment.[4]

Thirdly, 'We give aid because in the widest sense we believe it to be in our interest to do so as a member of the world community. We recognize that it is in the nature of aid that we should accept an economic sacrifice when giving it.'[5] Though most of Britain's aid is given through bilateral arrangements, 10 per cent of the aid programme for 1964–5 was on multilateral aid as 'the most direct recognition of the fact that our own aid programme is part of a great international movement to promote the development of non-industrialized countries'. The ideas of sacrifice and of an international movement for peace and progress have appealed to youth both in Britain and America.

It was the late President Kennedy of the United States who fired the imagination of youth throughout the world when in his inaugural address on January 20th, 1961, he said:

To those people in the huts and villages of half the globe struggling to break the bonds of mass misery, we pledge our best efforts to help them help themselves, for whatever period is required—not because the Communists may be doing it, not because we seek their votes, but because it is right. If a free society cannot help the many who are poor, it cannot save the few who are rich.

Two months later, he asked Congress to establish a new organization, the Agency for International Development (AID) charged to launch a Decade of Development 'on which will depend substantially the kind of world in which we and our children shall live'.

For this Decade of Development the United Nations General Assembly set as a target that by the end of the decade the income of the developing countries should grow at the rate of at least 5 per cent a year; and although the Specialized Agencies of the United Nations, the Food and Agriculture Organization, UNESCO, the U.N. Relief and Works Agency, the World Food Programme, the U.N. Children's Fund, the Expanded Programme of Technical Assistance, and Special Fund are all helping the developing countries, they are still far from the set target, and more aid is demanded.

The reasons for the United States AID programmes are given as follows:

Since the Second World War, the United States has conducted programmes of economic and military assistance to other countries in recognition of the fact that our own security depends, in large degree, on the strength of other free nations, and in affirmation of our moral conviction that the rich should help the poor.

In those nations where other people are willing to defend their independence against Communist aggression or subversion, where the governments and their citizens are trying to eradicate poverty, misery, and disease, it is plainly in our interest to help. A world of independent nations able to secure a decent measure of economic and social progress for their people is the kind of world in which our own freedom and our own hopes are safest.[6]

In his first address to a joint session of Congress, President Lyndon Johnson reaffirmed America's determination to carry on the fight against poverty and misery, ignorance and disease in other lands as well as in the United States.

As far as Africa is concerned, the United States has regarded her economic aid as subsidiary and supplementary to that provided by the Western European countries; even so, U.S. aid and loans to Africa for the years 1948–63 totalled $1,349.6 million; the total for 1963 was $266 million, two-thirds of which went to Liberia, Nigeria, and Tunisia. The emphasis is on self-help by the recipient countries which are expected to take the difficult measures necessary to ensure economic growth. Through Development Loans and Technical Assistance, the United States has joined in building houses, roads, railways, and dams; and in launching various productive enterprises. Much help has been given in education—in elementary and secondary schools, in universities, in adult education and vocational training; in health and public works, and in public administration. Since 1961, Peace Corps Volunteers have helped in all these fields in cities and villages and rural areas.

France is the biggest donor of aid to Africa, through contributions in finance and personnel, both military and civil, to the former French colonies, many of whom still maintain close ties with France. There are many joint enterprises, and French personnel in schools, in administration, in commerce and industry, military and police, and other public services sustain the French-speaking African States. There are some who could hardly carry on if France withdrew her support. It can be said that the pace of develop-

L

ment in Africa has depended very largely on aid from the Western countries and America.

But the whole question of aid has been complicated by the Cold War. As we have noted, the Soviet Union warns African countries against receiving aid from the Western countries, because it could be imperialism, or 'neo-colonialism' via grants and loans to control African countries, and destroy their newly won independence. America, on the other hand, warns against Communism being introduced by the Soviet Union via aid and cultural agreements to smother the freedom of Africa. China now warns against accepting aid from the Soviet Union because the Russians are 'white', and are allies of the American 'imperialists' to exploit Africans. Russia warns against China as an apostle of revolution, and America warns against subversion by both. Events in Africa have justified some of these warnings; others have been found to be baseless; but together, they have created an atmosphere of suspicion and mistrust, so that aid, whether in terms of grants or loans, or technical assistance, or selfless humanitarianism, has become suspect, and is making only a small contribution towards the sense of world community for which it is promoted.

The countries of Africa consider that the atmosphere would be improved, if all the donor countries would pool their aid so that it would all be multilateral—a joint international effort for peace and progress; but the donor countries, on their part, prefer bilateral arrangements; some make what amounts only to token contributions to the multilateral agencies, and others, particularly of the Eastern bloc, refuse to do even that; consequently, the countries of Africa have found it necessary to be cautious to preserve their independence through a policy of 'neutralism' and non-alignment. Some have gone beyond this, and have entered the ideological war to the extent of calling donor countries neo-colonialists, or accusing them of imperialist designs while taking aid from them, as President Nkrumah has done in his book *Neo-Colonialism, the last stage of Imperialism*, where he accused America of being the foremost 'neo-colonialist' power intent on exploiting African nations, and attacked American agencies responsible for the distribution of aid, such as the Peace Corps.[7] This drew a protest from the American Assistant-Secretary of State for African Affairs through the Ghanaian Ambassador in Washington. Since 1956, Ghana has received $166,500,000 (£59,500,000) under the United States Aid programme. United States aid to Ghana is currently running at $3.2 million a year: $1 million through charitable organizations, $1.2 million for technical assistance, and $1 million for the resettlement of 80,000 people moved from their homes because of the Volta Dam project. We have also referred to warnings by African leaders against Chinese subversion, based on their experience of Chinese activities in their own territories. The reverberations of the ideological battles of the Cold War are, in fact, hindering progress on some of the complex problems of aid.

Recipient countries want aid 'without strings attached' in order to preserve their independence and sovereignty; but donor countries have to justify aid to their taxpayers, and it would be irresponsible on their part to give aid without conditions; especially when experience has shown that aid to some countries has been misused by persons in authority for their own benefit, instead of the welfare of their people, as was intended; more important, the principal object of aid, namely, world peace and stability, would be defeated if aid continued to be given to authoritarian governments whose oppressive measures at home threaten stability and the wider peace of the world. There needs to be some frank exchanges, based on courageous loyalty to declared aims, to create a better atmosphere of confidence in which the justifiable fears of recipient countries will be allayed, and the undeniable responsibilities of donor countries appreciated.

Africa needs much more aid than she is receiving, if the target rate set for economic growth is to be attained; moreover, difficult problems have already arisen over the aid she has received. In some cases, it has been difficult to service the loans that have been given; and there is also the low and fluctuating prices of agricultural crops on the world markets, causing a widening gap between the donor countries and the recipient countries. Every African country would like the donor countries to make it possible for the agricultural products of Africa to earn more foreign exchange through agreements which would ensure higher and more stable price levels, so that they can pay their debts and maintain the target level of development. There is another foreseeable problem as a consequence of development. If the aid which has already been given is successful, it will mean that some African countries will soon need markets for their manufactured goods. Will the economic groups of business and labour organizations whose interests may be affected be prepared for the necessary changes in international trade to be made? The creation of a world community through interdependence will require bigger sacrifices from recipients and donors alike. The atmosphere of mistrust and suspicion will need to be cleared. This is why the problem of development and aid is rightly seen to be a moral problem; one element is the creation of mutual confidence, of which there is little at present. Emotive political slogans and accusations have to give way to constructive co-operation.

Aid from the industrialized countries to the developing States of Africa is a symbol of the embryonic world community. In addition, there is evidence of the search of African States for union. There have been a number of short-lived groupings, but the underlying desire for union has persisted. The first of the post-independence groupings was the Ghana–Guinea Union of November 23rd, 1958, which was expected to be the nucleus of a wider union. On May 1st, 1959, Sekou Touré and Kwame Nkrumah signed a document stating the 'Basic Principles of the Union of Independent African States'. They envisaged union citizenship, an Economic Council of the Union, and a Union Bank. The intentions did not materialize. Senegal and Soudan formed the Mali Federation in April 1959, but it broke up in August 1960; and the Soudan which retained the name Mali, joined Ghana and Guinea to form a Union of the three States on December 24th, 1960, 'to promote a common economic and monetary policy'. That Union, too, has remained only on paper.

The Conseil de l'Entente of Ivory Coast, Upper Volta, Niger, and Dahomey was formed in the middle of 1959 for mutual co-operation in economic affairs, in rail and road transport, postal services. and customs. The four States established their headquarters in Ouagadougou, in Upper Volta, where they built an imposing Council Hall and residences for their meetings. They have operated a joint development fund, and with growing understanding and cordiality they have extended their co-operation in the economic field into the political. Togo joined the Entente in

1965. In January 1966 the member states of the Conseil de l'Entente agreed on the principle of dual nationality. This would have meant that a citizen of any one of the countries could, in whichever of the others he resided, enjoy the same rights of citizenship as the natives of the country. It was a step in the direction of political union, resulting from economic co-operation. But the citizens of the Ivory Coast expressed fears that they might be faced on their own home-ground with fierce competition for jobs by nationals of the other countries of the Entente. President Houphonet Boigny therefore decided to limit the application of dual nationality in the Ivory Coast to citizens of the 'brother countries' of the Entente 'who have struggled with us, fought with us, are established here, and who voted in the Legislative and Presidential elections of November 7th, 1965'. The limitation that the Ivory Coast has had to impose confirms the lesson of previous attempts at political unions that the search for union has brighter prospects when it is approached through economic co-operation, provided the richer members are prepared to help the poorer ones, and that greater difficulties are encountered in the political field.

The groupings of the French-speaking States which have been functional associations based on economic co-operation have survived, whereas political unions and federations have failed, or have even not got off the ground. The Afro-Malagasy Union of twelve former French countries formed in March 1961, which came to be referred to as the 'Brazzaville Powers' or UAM (Union Africaine et Malagache) survived because of its co-operation in defence and economic affairs, including the running of a joint airline, Air Afrique. It was dissolved along with the 'Cassablanca' grouping of Ghana, Guinea, Mali, Morocco, and the United Arab Republic, and the 'Monrovia' Powers which comprised Cameroon, the Central African Republic, Chad, Congo (Brazzaville), Congo (Leopoldville), Dahomey, Ethiopia, Gabon, Ivory Coast, Liberia, Malagasy, Mauretania, Niger, Senegal, Sierra Leone, Somalia, Togo, Tunisia, and Upper Volta, when the Organization of African Unity (OAU), which came into existence in 1961, passed a resolution calling for the dissolution of regional political organizations. The UAM then became the Union Africaine et Malagache pour la Coopération Economique. It thus fulfilled the OAU resolution, but the metamorphosis revealed the real interests which bound the members together.

At a meeting held in February 1965 in Nouakchott, the capital of Mauretania, attended by the heads of all the French-speaking African States, with the exception of Guinea and Mali, it was decided to create the Organisation Commune Africaine et Malagache (OCAM) with its headquarters and secretariat at Yaounde in Cameroon. The communique announcing the formation of the organization showed that the fourteen States that formed it had political as well as economic objectives. There were significant references to 'non-interference in the domestic affairs' of other States. This, it was stated, as a 'sine qua non' of peace and development in Africa. It attacked the subversion organized by certain States, 'notably Ghana', who welcomed agents of subversion and organized training camps in their territories. These statements in the communique showed some of the dangers that threatened African Unity. Earlier, President Senghor had written that the actual deeds of independent African governments contradict their pan-African declarations. As soon as independence is acquired, most African States, still afflicted by European viruses, begin to secrete a conquering imperialism. They argue over their present borders, claim portions of neighbouring territories, maintain in their countries, at considerable expense, emigrants and shadow governments or, in other countries, subsidize fifth columns in their service. I do not see how one can possibly create the United States of Africa if one starts by disuniting the States of the Continent, if one does not begin by respecting their integrity and their frontiers.[11]

President Nkrumah whom the Nouakchott communiqué attacked is the campaigner for the immediate political union of all African States. The other leaders regard this as impracticable, though their membership in the Organization of African Unity attests to their common support for Union as an ultimate objective. When at the OAU meeting held in Cairo in July 1964, President Nkrumah spoke about Pan-Africanism, and put his case for immediate political union as the only way for Africa, President Nyerere said in his speech replying:

At one time I used to think that we all genuinely wanted a Continental Government of Africa; that the major difference between us was how to bring it about. I am afraid I am beginning to doubt this earlier assessment of mine. I am becoming increasingly convinced that we are divided between those who genuinely want a Continental Government and will patiently work for its realization, removing the obstacles, one by one; and those who simply use a phrase 'Union Government' for the purpose of propaganda. . . .

We do not believe there is a choice between achieving African Unity step by step and achieving it in one act. The one act choice is not available except in some curious imagination.

President Nkrumah again urged immediate African Union at the OAU Conference held in Accra in October 1965. Again, he did not win support. The consensus of opinion was that the time was not ripe for a Continental Union Government, but the Conference avoided a decision and asked the matter to be brought up at its next meeting in Addis Ababa. Some heads of State of OCAM, including all heads of State of the Entente, boycotted the Accra meeting, in protest against alleged subversion directed against their States from Ghana.

Although OCAM has formulated political aims, it is held together by its economic interests. The marketing of raw materials was the principal topic discussed at the meeting of its Foreign Ministers held in January 1966 in Tananarive, Madagascar. The Foreign Ministers agreed to recommend to the heads of States plans for the joint marketing of sugar which, if successful, will be followed by similar schemes for the marketing of groundnuts, cotton, and other raw materials.

The members of OCAM have repeatedly insisted that their organization is not a threat to the wider Organization of African Unity which has taken the place of the rival political groupings of Africa; but their existence shows that progress towards political union has better prospects if it proceeds by stages through co-operation on economic projects. This gives significance to the work of the United Nations Economic Commission for Africa (ECA) which is encouraging the establishment of regional ventures, and the rationalization of economic projects on a regional basis. Multinational co-operation is essential for efficiency and for economic growth at the rate the United Nations has set itself. It could also undergird political union. The agreement reached in 1963 to establish an African Development Bank was thus a decision of major importance, since its establishment will help to finance more regional projects. The Organization for African Unity may find itself treading the path the European Economic Community set out to tread: to reach political union through economic co-operation; regional co-operation on economic projects could lead to political union.

Brotherhood needs to be expressed in mutual aid in the fight against poverty, ignorance and disease; in tackling together the common problems of development. The improvement of living standards is a major task on which all can co-operate. It will help to create the framework within which freedom can have a real meaning, and union a sound foundation. It is through co-operation for development that the right attitudes for a political union can be inculcated, and the most appropriate institutions discovered.

It was on October 27th, 1964, that the British Government stated that a declaration of independence by Rhodesia 'would be an open act of defiance and rebellion, and it would be treasonable to take steps to give effect to it'. In spite of this, barely two months later, Mr. Ian Smith declared the independence of Rhodesia. The strength of African feeling against this may be seen from the fact that a meeting of the Foreign Ministers of the Organization of African Unity unanimously agreed to recommend to their heads of State to break off diplomatic relations with Britain if Mr. Smith was not ousted by December 15th, 1965. Not all heads of State accepted this recommendation, but Tanzania, Ghana, the United Arab Republic, and Algeria have broken off diplomatic relations with Britain, because they think Britain should have resorted to sterner measures than sanctions.

White minority rule is a denial of racial equality and justice. All Africans are agreed that the continent should be free from vestiges of racial domination. News of the illegal Rhodesian régime, or of apartheid in South Africa, or about thousands of refugees from the Portuguese colony of Mozambique seeking shelter in Malawi and Zambia are all seen as aspects of the same issue: Africa's battle for racial equality.

Amidst the turbulence of Africa can be discerned the striving for social and economic justice, for racial equality, for true freedom for all in the community of nations. The ongoing search for development, for socialism, and for wider union, amounts to a search for a world in which every man can live a life of dignity in freedom. Social justice, freedom, and human dignity are all, as we have seen, ideals of democracy. Africa, and indeed, mankind, can unite in brotherhood in their pursuit towards the building of the peaceful world community which all desire.

CHAPTER TEN

Democracy is a Way of Life

We have looked at two views of democracy which we may call respectively, the Marxist–Leninist view and the 'Western' view.

The Marxist–Leninist concept presents democracy as absolute rule by the majority in the form of the dictatorship of the proletariat under the leadership of the 'vanguard of the proletariat'. In this view, civil liberties are merely parts of the 'superstructure' of the State, formal and without substance, as long as the means of production are not owned by the State. When the State does own the means of production under the dictatorship of the proletariat, then the total life of the individual becomes the concern of the State; his family life, his leisure, his sport, and all his political and economic activities are under State direction; no sphere of life is outside the ambit and concern of the State.

In the Western concept of democracy, there used to be efforts to confine the actions of the State within narrow political limits, and to try to define sacrosanct spheres of life into which the State may not intrude. A remarkable development in the twentieth century has been the general acceptance of the broadening of the concept to include all activities of life. Contemporary ideas go beyond political

equality, and even equality of economic opportunity. Increasingly, the idea of the Welfare State is being linked
with democracy; with the conception that the young should
have proper care and education; that adults should have
employment, decent social conditions and leisure; that there
should be minimum standards of living beyond which no
one should be allowed to fall; that the sick, the aged, and the
handicapped should be looked after; there is no aspect of
life, not even family life, that is regarded as outside the
sphere of the democratic State; it is now accepted that the
State should be concerned with the total life of the individual from the cradle to the grave.

The fundamental difference between the two concepts is
how the concern is shown, and how the inroads of the State
upon one's life are made. The Western model, as we have
seen, provides for more effective safeguards against tyranny.
It shows concern for individual freedom and initiative. In
either case, it is more true today than ever before to describe
democracy as a way of life, concerned with all the institutions and activities of society.

We have seen how concerned the State is with the
economic life of the people. All African States are waging a
battle against poverty. This is reflected in their development
plans. We have discussed their need for help from the
richer countries, and the response the latter are making
through various forms of aid which are given not as charity
but as international co-operation for the mutual benefit of
donor and recipient.

We have referred to the democratic idea that there should
be equality of opportunity, economic as well as political.
Within each State, the government is expected to take
measures which will ensure a steady increase in the nation's

wealth, and in its equitable distribution. The desire for social justice underlies the various concepts of socialism. We have observed that socialism is not identical with democracy, and there is already enough evidence in Africa to show its pitfalls. There are countries which, despite the avowal of socialism, have failed to ensure equitable distribution, or check corruption; consequently, there is a growing inequality between the mass of the population and the privileged party and government officers; moreover, the concentration of political and economic power in the same hands has been used to curb the freedom of individuals as well as of associations.

The efforts to achieve economic growth have shown that success depends not only on the government but also on the work which everyone does, and how he does it. The policeman on his beat, braving danger in order that others may sleep in peace and safety; the farmer in his fields, clearing, sowing, harvesting; the shopkeeper in his shop serving many customers; the clerk working late, or the workman in the factory toiling overtime so that orders may be fulfilled; the lorry driver conveying goods or people from place to place; the technician, labourer, or government official at his allotted task; the parliamentarian in the legislature, or Bench and Bar in the Courts; the doctor in his surgery, or the nurse at the patient's bedside—the success of democracy depends on the discipline, the efficiency, the honesty, and the courtesy which they show in the discharge of their duties and in their day to day relations with the public. Their activities are all part of the quality of social life with which democracy is concerned.

The basic unit of social life is the family, which, in Africa, calls for greater concern than elsewhere. As we have indicated, African concepts of man see him primarily as a member of a family which includes broadening extensions of kinship structures from the nuclear unit of husband, wife, and children to the tribe. The solidarity of traditional kinship structures is a value which is widely desired for the heterogeneous groupings of the new nations; at the same time, tribal loyalties which are expressions of that solidarity have posed problems for nation-building. We have suggested that where the tribe is a geographical unit, it is possible to solve many of the problems by development and devolution. New nations can find unity in diversity; and people of one tribe can learn to accept those of another tribe on equal terms, as fellow citizens.

Family and kinship structures command attention for other important reasons. The home is the place where through informal education, ideas, attitudes, and habits are acquired; democratic patterns of behaviour can be fostered or discouraged there. Then there is formal education in which parents as well as governments are interested; parents, because they desire a safe and happy life for their children; and governments, because the young are the citizens of tomorrow. Governments want the young to be taught the skills needed for national development, and the ways of good citizenship.

All African governments have given education a high priority and spend large proportions of their available resources on it. They accept education as an investment for future prosperity.

It is not only democratic governments that are interested in education; totalitarian and authoritarian régimes see education as an important and useful tool. They are noted for controlling educational institutions and adapting them so that they inculcate subservience and fear, and the appropriate indoctrination to ensure that the young give fanatic and unquestioning loyalty, often including the 'personality cult' and deification of the leader. Would-be dictators do not leave educational institutions free.

There are various other social questions which make education an urgent concern for African governments. African communities have high rates of illiteracy. When a country is in that situation, universal adult suffrage, the much demanded 'one man, one vote' does not necessarily mean democracy; it is a condition which can result in rule by a literate oligarchy. The faster literacy and education can be spread, the better the prospects for democracy.

Another important and general social question concerns the present state of the institution of the family. Along with other social changes, such as commerce and industry, education has caused changes in occupations and in family relationships. Traditional obligations and reciprocities now impose heavy burdens on those who are in regular, gainful employment. The family is no longer able to provide security for all its members. This is another reason why responsible governments must be concerned with the family. They are expected to provide for the sick, the aged, and the unemployed for whom even the extended family is no longer able to cater. There are many pressures and strains on the institution of the family amidst social change; it is still resilient, but it cannot cope with all the burdens which rapid social changes have imposed on it.

Through various voluntary associations based on common interests rather than blood ties, people seek to provide for the interests and needs which they can no longer obtain from what used to be the all-embracing web of kinship relations. These voluntary associations can be a training ground for good citizenship. They may be economic associations like trade unions or traders' associations, or educational like youth or People's Educational associations, or benevolent associations of which many kinds have sprung up. Democratic governments usually respect the independence of such associations and where necessary they provide the constitutional framework within which they can function and pursue their objectives; but authoritarian régimes seek to curb or swallow up all such associations in a monolithic single party. In the democratic society, the associations are recognized as promoting one interest or other, or of safeguarding one form of liberty or another; but authoritarian régimes see them as undesirable sources of independent power to be checked in the interest of 'social order'.

Social order does not rest on the imposition of restraints; but democracy demands that these should be as few as possible; it demands toleration and freedom of action; it seeks to prevent certain evils, the principal among them being dictatorship. Consequently, appropriate institutions are developed and fostered for the taming of power; for subjecting those who rule to constant criticism and checks. Among these institutions, as we saw in Chapter Six, are the party system, the organized opposition, the press, the Rule of Law, and the independent Judiciary.

In our review, we have presented evidence of the general desire for democracy. The new States of Africa are, however, in quest of appropriate institutions through which to express the democratic values they avow. In particular, many of them consider the institutions of opposition as established within Western political systems to be unsuitable for their communities. Democracy allows experimentation and innovation, for one of its demands is the readiness to compromise. We have, nevertheless, questioned whether the single-party experiments provide adequately for criticism and opposition. There is a need for new attitudes to the expression of criticism, and for the establishment and recognition of institutions through which opposition can function adequately. A basic tenet of democracy, as we have stated, is that all men, including party bosses and rulers, are fallible, and consequently that there should be effective institutions for the expression of criticism, and for a constitutional change of rulers. Intolerance of opposition often stems from the conviction that the party bosses are always right, and that only they understand and interpret the will of the people; so that whatever they say should be accepted without challenge. Such an attitude is very dangerous for the democratic life. We have questioned the adequacy of criticism when it is allowed only within the single-party, since this presupposes that opposition must be confined within the limits set by the leadership, and the ideology and programme of the one party. Challenge to its basic presuppositions cannot be tolerated, for that would spell rancorous dissentions, and instability. There are strict limits to the non-conformist ideas that a party which must govern can tolerate. There are some, as we have shown, who are prepared to accept that what they are practising now falls short of the democratic principles they avow, but justify authoritarian practices as temporary and necessary expedients in their particular social context; the greater danger lies with those who seem prepared to defend their present experiments as the acme of democracy, despite its obvious shortcomings, and the sufferings they inflict on those who oppose or disagree with them. Hopefully, no human institutions can be static; there are already severe tensions which point compellingly to the need for continuing the quest for more appropriate forms.

The first chapter showed that the social institutions which men establish and maintain are related to their concepts of the universe, and to their philosophy of life. In traditional African concepts, as we saw, religion and life were inseparable. Religion defined moral duties and regulated conduct in all spheres of life, including the political sphere. We saw how the rejection of Communism, for example, is based in part on its teaching about religion which even Marxist African leaders have expressly repudiated. Religious freedom is respected in most African States, and the political institutions permit people of different faiths to practise and propagate their religion. Though most of Africa's educated leaders are either Moslem or Christian, traditional faiths also flourish. They give the best expressions of indigenous music and dance, and of graphic and plastic art forms which are increasingly prized, because they are among the most distinctive achievements which Africa brings as her contribution to the common inheritance of mankind. They are unique expressions of Africa's way of life.

It is not only cultural contributions that can be made to the common inheritance of mankind. Social co-operation is possible among peoples of different races and cultures for the achievement both of material well-being and of values which are capable of being recognized as universally good. This is why it is possible to have multi-racial associations like the Commonwealth or the United Nations. When nationals of one country send aid to relieve famine in another, or volunteers from one country go to another to teach or to administer to the sick, or when an international organization devotes itself to the freeing of those imprisoned for their political or religious convictions, we are given examples of a moral language which is universally understood.

It is our contention that democracy has a moral language capable of being universally understood, as the avowals of African leaders have clearly demonstrated in the foregoing pages. It is universally understood that imprisoning people without a fair trial, because the religious or political opinions they hold displease those in authority is wrong; that the denial of the basic freedoms which have repeatedly been pronounced by different leaders in different countries, such as the right to life, the freedom of expression, or association, or movement, and the like is unjust. All men suffer from oppression, and abhor and condemn it. In this, too, they speak a common language.

This does not mean that all democratic societies must have the same political institutions. The things we have observed in this summary to be the concerns of democracy : the raising of living standards, seeking a fair distribution of a nation's wealth, devising means to give equality of opportunity to all, or to protect the rights of individuals and associations, developing institutions which will curb the rulers and make the consent of the governed meaningful and effective, and allow maximum freedom for individual and social life, express universal cravings. But the institutions which each country devises to give effect to them are various; they constitute a country's way of life. Democracy reflects the history, the culture, and the values of each country; it is revealed in the day to day life and activities of the society; in the relations between government and opposition; in social relations in the home, in the school, in public places; in the general moral atmosphere of the society, and in the quality of the individual citizen; for democracy, more than other forms of government is the expression of faith in the individual; a democratic society relies more on the judgment, self-discipline, sense of responsibility, and the freely given loyalty of its citizens to the moral principles on which its system ultimately rests.

All peoples can achieve and practise democracy, if they have enough faith and conviction in its values. It is not for the European only; it has a moral language which is universal. Those who have the courage, and enough respect for the African to point out the shortcomings of contemporary political experiments, as measured against the accepted and avowed standards, perform a valuable service for democracy as well as for Africa; those who fall over backwards, whether out of desire to please, or fear to give offence, or contempt for the African, to defend the shortcomings and represent them as the best that can be achieved are being pernicious both to the freedom and welfare of African societies and to international relations and world peace.

The ideals of democracy set challenging goals to each generation, and the response of each generation can be seen in the institutions it passes on to succeeding generations. To argue that no country is fully democratic, as some have done in order to excuse oppressive practices, is to misunderstand the nature of a political society that evinces faith in democracy; such a society is the theatre of man's constant striving for better social justice, and for a wider and wider scope for the development of individual and social life in dignity and freedom. Democracy is the expression of faith in man's capacity for the progressive extension of freedom and justice in society.

We may appropriately end with an old Chinese story:

In passing by the side of Mount Thai, Confucius came on a woman who was weeping bitterly by a grave. The Master pressed forward and drove quickly to her; then he sent Tze-lu to question her. 'Your wailing,' said he, 'is that of one who has suffered sorrow on sorrow.' She replied, 'That is so. Once my husband's father was killed here by a tiger. My husband was also killed, and now my son has died in the same way.' The Master said, 'Why do you not leave the place?' The answer was, 'There is no oppressive government here.' The Master then said, 'Remember this, my children: oppressive government is more terrible than tigers.'[1]

'Freedom!' was the battle-cry against colonialism in Africa; the next stage is to free the continent from oppressive government. It is a task which belongs to the present generation, and to our successors.

References

CHAPTER ONE: THE RELIGIOUS HERITAGE

1. *On African Socialism* (Frederick A. Praeger, 1964), p. 26.
2. Sessional Paper No. 10 of 1963/5, para. 10.
3. Senghor, *op. cit.*, pp. 93-4.
4. *African Worlds*, International African Institute (O.U.P., 1954).
5. Rattray: *Ashanti Proverbs* (The Clarendon Press, Oxford, 1916), p. 20.
6. Brodie Cruickshank, *Eighteen Years on The Gold Coast of Africa* (Hurst and Blackett, London, 1853), Vol. II, pp. 153-4.
7. Senghor, *op. cit.*, p. 46.
8. Sessional Paper No. 10 of 1963/5, para. 16.

CHAPTER TWO: THE POLITICAL HERITAGE

1. H. S. Maine, *Lectures on the Early History of Institutions* (New York, 1888), pp. 72-4.
2. Republic of Kenya: Sessional Paper No. 10 of 1963/5, para. 11.
3. *African Political Systems*, M. Fortes and E. E. Evans-Pritchard (eds.) (O.U.P., 1940).
4. *African Political Systems*, p. 5.

5. Brodie Cruickshank, *Eighteen Years on the Gold Coast of Africa* (London, 1854).
6. Republic of Kenya: Sessional Paper No. 10 of 1963/5, para. 9.

CHAPTER THREE: COLONIALISM

1. Senghor, *African Socialism*, p. 36.
2. Kimble, *Tropical Africa*, Vol. II, p. 157.
3. Field, *Search for Security*, p. 30 (Faber & Faber, 1960).
4. Field, *op. cit.*, p. 32.
5. *Black Orpheus*, 1958.
6. Translated in *Mizan Newsletter*, Vol. 6, No. 3, March 1964.
7. Potekhin, *op. cit.*
8. See, for example, Brodie Cruickshank, *Eighteen Years on the Gold Coast of Africa*.

CHAPTER FOUR: COMMUNIST PRESCRIPTIONS FOR DEMOCRACY

1. *The U.S.S.R. and Africa*, David Morrison, pp. 10–14.
2. *Mizan Newsletter*, Vol. 3, No. 1, January 1961.
3. *Ibid.*
4. *Pravda*, January 5th, 1961.
5. Sivolov, The National Liberation Movement in *Mizan Newsletter*, Vol. 3, No. 6, June 1961.
6. *Africa*, Moscow, 1961; *Alya I Afrika Segondnya*, No. 10, 1961, cited in *Mizan Newsletter*, Vol. 4, No. 1, January 1962.
7. Potekhin, article in *Kommunist*, No. 1, 1964, pp. 104–13. *Mizan Newsletter*, Vol. 6, No. 3, March 1964.
8. *Mizan Newsletter*, Vol. 5, No. 10, November 1963.
9. *Mizan Newsletter*, Vol. 5, No. 4, April 1963.
10. *West African Pilot*, January 2nd, 1961.

11. *Mezhdunarodnaya Zhizn,* No. 1, 1963, *Mizan Newsletter,* Vol. 5, No. 2, February 1963.
12. *Kommunist,* No. 1, 1964, pp. 104–13.
13. *Sovetskaya Etnografiya,* No. 6, 1960; and No. 1, 1961.
14. *Mizan Newsletter,* Vol. 1, No. 4, January 1962.

CHAPTER FIVE: AFRICAN CONCEPTS OF SOCIALISM

1. Republic of Kenya: Sessional Paper No. 10 of 1963/5, paras. 7–11.
2. The address was published in April 1962 by the Tanganyika African National Union, and has since appeared as an Appendix in *African Socialism,* edited by William Friedland and Carl Rosberg Jr. (Stanford University Press, 1964), pp. 238–47.
3. Referred to in Chapter Three.
4. 'The Foreign Policy of Mali', in *International Affairs,* London, Vol. 38, No. 4, October 1961, pp. 436–7.
5. *Ujamaa, op. cit.,* p. 246.
6. *Op. cit.,* Sessional Paper, para. 10.
7. *Op. cit.,* Sessional Paper, para. 36.
8. *Ujamaa, op. cit.,* p. 246.
9. Senghor, *African Socialism,* p. 77.
10. *The Spark,* April 19th, 1963.
11. Nkrumah, *Consciencism* (London, Heinemann, 1964).
12. *Op. cit.,* Sessional Paper, para. 142 (c).
13. *Op. cit.,* Sessional Paper, para. 77.
14. *Op. cit.,* Sessional Paper, para. 4.
15. Culled from *Le Monde,* December 31st, 1965.
16. *Op cit.,* Sessional Paper, para. 101.
17. *Ujamaa, op. cit.,* p. 246.
18. Senghor, *African Socialism,* p. 33.
19. *Ujamaa, op. cit.,* p. 242.

M

20. Socialist International Information (London), XI, No. 18, May 6th, 1961, pp. 276–7.
21. Hugh Seton-Watson: *The New Imperialism* (The Bodley Head, London, 1961).

CHAPTER SIX: THE INGREDIENTS OF DEMOCRACY

1. Quoted by Aimé Cesaire in 'The Political Thought of Sekou Touré', *Présence Africaine*, No. 29, 1960.
2. *Zik. A selection from the speeches of Nnamdi Azikiwe* (Cambridge University Press, 1961), pp. 97–8.
3. 'The New Constitution of Nigeria and the Protection of Human Rights and Fundamental Freedoms' by Dr. T. O. Elias in *Journal of International Commission of Jurists*, Vol. 2. No. 2, 1960.
4. *Bulletin of the International Commission of Jurists*, No. 14, October 1962.
5. President Olympio in *Africa Speaks* (Van Nostrand, Princeton, N.J., 1961), pp. 76–7.
6. 'The New Constitution of Morocco' in *Bulletin of the International Commission of Jurists*, No. 16, July 1963, pp. 28–36.
7. Reported in *The Times*, July 7th, 1962.
8. *Journal of International Commission of Jurists*, Vol. 3, No. 1, Spring 1961, pp. 23–4.
9. *Journal of International Commission of Jurists*, Vol. 1, No. 1, August 1957, p. 6.
10. *Proceedings of the African Conference on the Rule of Law*, published by the International Commission of Jurists, Geneva 1961.
11. *Journal of the International Commission of Jurists*, Vol. 2, No. 2, p. 3.
12. *Bulletin of International Commission of Jurists*, No. 12, November 1961, p. 50.

13. *Bulletin of the International Commission of Jurists*, No. 16, July 1963, pp. 25–6.
14. *Bulletin of the International Commission of Jurists*, No. 18, March 1964, pp. 9–13.
15. Reported in *The Times*, June 30th, 1962.
16. Vision of Africa in *Africa Speaks*, 1961, pp. 24–5.

CHAPTER SEVEN: TRIBALISM

1. M. Fortes and E. E. Evans-Pritchard, *African Political Systems*, pp. 1–24.
2. S. N. Eisenstadt, *From Generation to Generation* (Routledge and Kegan Paul, London, 1956), p. 120.
3. Reported in *The Guardian*, January 29th, 1966.
4. K. O. Dike, *Trade and Politics in the Niger Delta* (O.U.P., 1956), p. 44.
5. R. Emerson, *From Empire to Nation* (Harvard University Press, 1960), p. 103.
6. Aristide R. Zollberg, *One-Party Government in the Ivory Coast* (Princeton University Press, 1964), pp. 47–8.
7. K. A. Busia, *A Social Survey of Sekondi-Takoradi* (Crown Agents, London, 1950).
8. Philip J. Foster, *Education and Social Change in Ghana* (Routledge and Kegan Paul, London, 1965), p. 301.
9. Unesco, *Social Implications of Industrialization and Urbanization in Africa South of the Sahara* (1956).
10. Zollberg, *op. cit.* p. 62.
11. *Ibid.*, p. 286.
12. *Ibid.*, p. 116.
13. *Ibid.*, p. 296.
14. Gabriel A. Almond and James S. Coleman, *The Poltics of the Developing Areas* (Princeton University Press, 1960), p. 301.

CHAPTER EIGHT: DEMOCRACY AND ONE-PARTY SYSTEMS

1. W. Arthur Lewis; *Politics in West Africa* (G. Allen & Unwin, London, 1965), pp. 34–5.
2. *Op. cit.*, p. 63.
3. Reported in the *New York Times*, February 12th, 1960.
4. Reported in *The Guardian*, February 3rd, 1964.
5. *Bulletin of International Commission of Jurists*, No. 18, March 1964, p. 10.
6. *Journal of the International Commission of Jurists*, Vol. 3. No. 2, Winter 1961, pp. 65–81.
7. Tanganyika, *One-Party Commission Report*, p. 30.
8. *Ibid.*, p. 14.
9. *Ibid.*, p. 20.
10. *Ibid.*, p. 16.
11. *Ibid.*, p. 18.
12. *Ibid.*, p. 30.
13. *Ibid.*, p. 31.
14. *Ibid.*, p. 31.
15. *West Africa*, January 29th, 1966, p. 114.

CHAPTER NINE: THE SEARCH FOR UNION AND WORLD
BROTHERHOOD

1. Reported in *West African Pilot*, January 29th, 1966.
2. *Overseas Development*, Cmnd. 2736. (London, H.M.S.O., August 1965), p. 6.
3. *Ibid.*, p. 6.
4. *Ibid.*, p. 7.
5. *Ibid.*, p. 7.
6. *Proposed Mutual Defense and Development Programs FY 1965*, Summary Presentation to Congress, April 1964, p. 1.
7. Kwame Nkrumah, *Neo-colonialism: The Last Stage of Imperialism* (T. Nelson, London, 1965), Introduction, *passim*.

8. *Realités Ivoiriennes*, Paris, No. 13, January 28th 1966, p. 3.
9. *Ibid.*, p. 4.
10. Zollberg, *One-Party Government in the Ivory Coast*, pp. 336–7.
11. Leopold Sedar Senghor, *African Socialism*, p. 91.

CHAPTER TEN: DEMOCRACY IS A WAY OF LIFE

1. Bertrand Russell, *Power: A New Social Analysis* (G. Allen & Unwin, London, 1938), p. 285.

Index